ITIL® V3 Foundation Exam - The Study Guide

# Other publications by Van Haren Publishing

Van Haren Publishing (VHP) specializes in titles on Best Practices, methods and standards within four domains:
  - IT management
  - Architecture (Enterprise and IT)
  - Business management and
  - Project management

Van Haren Publishing offers a wide collection of whitepapers, templates, free e-books, trainer material etc. in the **VHP Freezone**: freezone.vanharen.net

VHP is also publisher on behalf of leading organizations and companies:
ASLBiSL Foundation, CA, Centre Henri Tudor, Gaming Works, Getronics, IACCM, IAOP, IPMA-NL, ITSqc, NAF, Ngi, PMI-NL, PON, Quint, The Open Group, The Sox Institute

Topics are (per domain):

| IT (Service) Management / IT Governance | Architecture (Enterprise and IT) | Project/Programme/ Risk Management |
|---|---|---|
| ABC of ICT | Archimate® | A4-Projectmanagement |
| ASL | GEA® | ICB / NCB |
| BiSL | SOA | MINCE® |
| CATS | TOGAF™ | M_o_R® |
| CMMI | | MSP™ |
| CoBIT | **Business Management** | P3O |
| ISO 17799 | CMMI | *PMBOK® Guide* |
| ISO 27001 | Contract Management | PRINCE2™ |
| ISO 27002 | EFQM | |
| ISO/IEC 20000 | eSCM | |
| ISPL | ISA-95 | |
| IT Service CMM | ISO 9000 | |
| ITIL® V3 | ISO 9001:2000 | |
| ITSM | OPBOK | |
| MOF | Outsourcing | |
| MSF | SAP | |
| SABSA | SixSigma | |
| | SOX | |

# ITIL® V3 Foundation Exam

## The Study Guide

# Colophon

| | |
|---|---|
| Title: | ITIL® V3 Foundation Exam - The Study Guide |
| Editors (Inform-IT): | Jan van Bon (Managing editor) |
| Authors: | Arjen de Jong |
| | Axel Kolthof |
| | Mike Pieper |
| | Ruby Tjassing |
| | Annelies van der Veen |
| | Tieneke Verheijen |
| Publisher: | Van Haren Publishing, Zaltbommel, www.vanharen.net |
| Design & layout: | CO2 Premedia bv, Amersfoort - NL |
| ISBN: | 978 90 8753 069 3 |
| Edition: | First edition, second impression with amendment, August 2009 |
| | First edition, third impression with minor amends, March 2011 |

# Foreword

This concise Study Guide provides details on the ITIL V3 Qualification Scheme, a practical introduction to the content of the five ITIL V3 core books, and an extensive set of exam questions to support the best exam preparation.

It explains the structure of the new Service Lifecycle in the context of IT service management principles, and explains what functions and processes are. Each of the phases in the Service Lifecycle is discussed in detail, including all functions and processes. Each chapter follows a standardized structure, and ends with a number of sample exam questions.

At the end of the guide, a full set of 40 sample questions of the ITIL V3 Foundation Exam is provided, including the answers to the sample questions.

The Study Guide provides detailed information on the ITIL V3 Foundation Exam and how to prepare for this exam. It also provides a cross-reference to the ITIL V3 Foundation Exam requirements, underpinning its value as an exam preparation tool.

This Study Guide contains Core ITIL material that is published under license from HMSO and was developed by a broad team of expert editors, expert authors and expert reviewers. It provides an essential tool for anyone taking the ITIL V3 Foundations Exam or the Version 2 to Version 3 Foundation Bridging exam.

It is based on the latest exam syllabus (4.2) and ITIL content, highlighting the areas needed to pass the exam. As a study aid it is ideal for those new to ITIL but also for those already familiar with ITIL V2, it is straight to the point, and provides you with an excellent reference to keep up to date.

Jan van Bon
Managing Editor ITSM Library

# Contents

## Appendices

# CHAPTER 1

# The ITIL® V3 Qualification Scheme[1]

## 1.1   About ITIL

The Information Technology Infrastructure Library™ (ITIL) offers a systematic approach to the delivery of quality IT services. ITIL was developed in the 1980s and 1990s by CCTA (Central Computer and Telecommunications Agency, now the **Office of Government Commerce, OGC**), under contract to the UK Government.

Since then, ITIL has provided not only a best practice based framework for IT management, but also an approach and philosophy shared by the people who work with it in practice. ITIL has now been updated twice, the first time in 2000-2002 (V2), and the second time in 2007 (V3). ITIL is supported by the **IT Service Management Forum (itSMF)**, an internationally recognized not-for-profit organization dedicated to support the development of IT service management, e.g. through publications in the ITSM Library series. It consists of a growing number of national chapters (50+), with itSMF International as the controlling body.

## 1.2   The ITIL® V3 Qualification Scheme

The ITIL V3 Qualification Scheme uses a system that enables an individual to gain credits for each exam they pass. Once candidates have accumulated a sufficient number of credits they can be awarded the ITIL Expert in IT Service Management. There are four levels within the scheme:
- Foundation Level
- Intermediate Level (Lifecycle Stream and Capability Stream)
- ITIL Expert
- ITIL Master

Figure 1.1 shows the structure of qualifications within the ITIL V3 scheme.

---

1   This chapter is based on text from the "ITIL Service Management Practices V3 Qualification Scheme 3.1", the website of APMG and the Official ITIL Site.

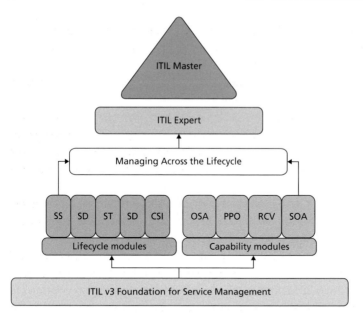

Figure 1.1 The ITIL V3 qualification scheme (Based on: OGC Source)

### 1.2.1   Foundation Level

The ITIL Foundation Certificate in IT service Management is targeted at:

- Individuals who require a basic understanding of the ITIL framework and how it may be used to enhance the quality of IT service management within an organization.
- IT professionals who are working within an organization that practices ITIL and who need to be informed about - and contribute to - service improvement.

The purpose of the ITIL Foundation Certificate in IT Service Management is to certify that the candidate has gained knowledge of the ITIL terminology, structure and basic concepts and has comprehended the core principles of ITIL practices for service management. More specifically, Foundation level candidates will have to gain knowledge and understanding of the following topics:

- **Service management as a practice** (Comprehension) - Define service and comprehend and explain the concept of service management as a practice.
- **Service lifecycle** (Comprehension) - Understand the service lifecycle and explain the objectives and business value for each phase in the lifecycle.

- **Key principles and models** (Comprehension) - Comprehend and account for the key principles and models of service management and 'the balance' of some opposing forces within service management.
- **Generic concepts** (Awareness) - Define some of the key terminology and explain the key concepts of service management.
- **Selected processes** (Awareness) - Understand how the service management processes contribute to the service lifecycle, explain the high level objectives, scope, basic concepts, activities, key metrics (KPI's), roles and challenges for five of the core processes and state the objectives, some of the basic concepts and roles for fifteen of the remaining processes.
- **Selected roles** (Awareness) - Account for the role and to be aware of the responsibilities of some of the key roles in service management and recognize a number of the remaining roles described in other learning units.
- **Selected functions** (Awareness) - Explain the role, objectives, organizational structures, staffing and metrics of the Service Desk function and state the role, objectives and overlap of three other functions.
- **Technology and architecture** (Awareness) - List some generic requirements for an integrated set of service management technology, and understand how service automation assists with integrating service management processes.
- **ITIL® V3 Qualification Scheme** (Awareness) - Explain the ITIL® V3 Qualification Scheme.

This list is not exhaustive. For more detailed information about the Foundation Exam topics, you can download the syllabus "The ITIL V3 Foundation Certificate in IT Service Management" at the official ITIL site (http://www.itil-officialsite.com), examine the cross-reference at the end of this book, or ask your accredited trainer.

### 1.2.2 Intermediate Level
There are two streams in the Intermediate level. Both streams assess an individual's ability to analyze and apply the concepts of ITIL. Candidates are able to take units from either of the Intermediate streams, to gain credits towards the Expert level.

- **Intermediate Lifecycle Stream** - This stream includes 5 individual certificates built around the five core OGC titles: Service Strategy, Service Design, Service Transition, Service Operation and Continual Service Improvement.
- **Intermediate Capability Stream** - This stream includes 4 individual certificates loosely based on the current V2 Clustered Practitioner qualifications, but broader in scope in line with the updated V3 content.

### 1.2.3 ITIL Expert

To achieve the ITIL Expert in IT Service Management, candidates must successfully complete a number of Intermediate units in addition to the mandatory Foundation level and the Managing Across The Lifecycle capstone course. This course brings together the full essence of a lifecycle approach to service management, and consolidates the knowledge gained across the qualification scheme.

### 1.2.4 ITIL Master

This level of the qualification will assess an individual's ability to apply and analyze the ITIL concepts in new areas. This higher level qualification is currently under development.

## 1.3 Examination Institutes

Professional qualifications based on ITIL are offered by Examination Institutes (EIs). An Examination Institute is an organization accredited by the APM Group (APMG) through the ITIL Qualifications Board. EIs are permitted to operate an ITIL examination scheme through a network of Accredited Training Organizations (ATOs), and Accredited Trainers with accredited materials. The Examination Institutes at the time of publication are listed below. The up-to-date list can be viewed on the APMG website.

### 1.3.1 APMG

APMG specialize in the accreditation and certification of organizations, processes and people. APMG are an ITIL Examination Institute, who offer global accreditation and examination services for training providers.

### 1.3.2 DANSK IT

DANSK IT is an interest organization for IT-professionals in Denmark. The core activities evolve around member networks, conferences, courses, certification programs and IT political advice to the Danish Government and its agencies. Founded in 1958 DANSK IT is among the first IT societies in the world.

### 1.3.3 DF Certifiering AB

DF Certifiering AB (DFC), is a wholly owned subsidiary to Dataföreningen i Sverige, the Swedish Computer Society with 26.000 IT professionals as members in Sweden. DFC's role is to give accreditation to training providers and certify IT. DFC also provide products in the field of information security and self-assessing tests for e-Citizens.

### 1.3.4  EXIN

The Examination Institute for Information Science in the Netherlands (EXIN) is a global, independent IT examination provider. EXIN establishes educational requirements and develops and organizes examinations and learning tracks in the field of IT.

### 1.3.5  ISEB

The Information Systems Examination Board (ISEB) is a wholly owned subsidiary of the British Computer Society. The ISEB provides industry recognized qualifications that measure competence, ability and performance in many areas of IT, including ITIL.

### 1.3.6  LCS

Loyalist Certification Services (LCS) is a premier deliverer of ITIL certification exams in North America.

## 1.4  Accredited Training Organizations

It is recommended that any training you receive is through an Accredited Training Organisation (ATO). Only ATOs and their affiliates have licences to offer training courses that incorporate official OGC trademarks, brands and copyrighted material. These ATOs have been fully accredited by an approved Examination Institute. The accreditation process involves an assessment of the organization's management systems, course materials and trainers, assuring the quality of training provided. The various Examination Institutes are in turn accredited by APMG, OGC's official accreditor.

The ATOs listed on the APMG website (http://www.apmgroup.co.uk) are accredited by the various Examination Institutes to provide training in ITIL.

## 1.5  About this Study Guide

This study guide is based on the ITSM Library publication: IT Service Management based on ITIL V3 - a Pocket Guide. For this publication, the content has been modified and updated to comply with the Foundation Examination specifications as defined in: "The INTERIM ITIL® V3 Foundation Certificate in IT Service Management SYLLABUS". **This guide is only intended as an aid** to help you pass your ITIL Foundation Exam, it is not an introduction to the ITIL core publications. For that purpose, please use: "Foundations of IT Service Management- based on ITIL V3", also published in the ITSM Library for itSMF International.

This study guide is set up in three parts. The first part introduces the service lifecycle in the context of IT service management principles, and explains what functions and processes are (Chapter 2).

The second part (Chapters 3 to 7) discusses each of the phases in the service lifecycle in more detail, including all functions and processes. Each chapter follows a standardized structure, and ends with a number of sample exam questions.

The third part of this guide (Chapter 8) provides more information on the ITIL V3 Foundation Exam and how to prepare for this exam. The chapter ends with a sample ITIL V3 Foundation Examination.

In the appendices of this guide you will find the answers to the sample questions, a cross-reference to the official ITIL V3 exam requirements, a list with acronyms, a glossary and a reference list.

CHAPTER 2

# Introduction

## 2.1 Definition of Service Management

ITIL is presented as "**good practice**". Good practice is an approach or method that has been proven in practice. Good practices can be a solid backing for organizations that want to improve their IT services.

The ITIL service lifecycle is based on ITIL's core concept of "service management" and the related concepts "service" and "value". These core terms in service management are explained as follows:
*   **Service management** - A set of specialized organizational capabilities for providing value to customers in the form of services.
*   **Service** - A means of delivering value to customers by facilitating outcomes the customers want to achieve without the ownership of specific costs or risks. Outcomes are possible from the performance of tasks and they are limited by a number of constraints. Services enhance performance and reduce the pressure of constraints. This increases the chances of the desired outcomes being realized.
*   **Value** - Value is the core of the service concept. From the customer's perspective, value consists of two core components: utility and warranty. Utility is what the customer receives, and warranty is how it is provided. The concepts "utility" and "warranty" are described in the Section "Service Strategy".

## 2.2 Service Management Technology

Technology plays a major role in IT service management. With the help of tools, management tasks can be automated, for example in monitoring tasks or software distribution tasks. Other tools support the performance of the activities themselves, for example help desk tools or service management tools.

An integrated set of service management technology should ideally include the following functionality:
*   support for all stages of the lifecycle
*   support for the design of services
*   self-help and remote control
*   an integrated Configuration Management System (CMS)

- technology for discovery/deployment/licensing/diagnostics/reporting
- dashboards

Automation is considered to improve utility and warranty of services (see section 3.2 for an explanation of the terms **utility** and **warranty**). Consider the following guidelines to prepare for automation:
- Simplify the processes before automating them.
- Clarify the flow of activities, allocation of tasks, need for information, and interactions.
- In self-service situations, reduce the surface area of contact users have with the underlying systems and processes.
- Do not hurry to automate tasks and interactions that are neither simple nor routine.

## 2.3   Overview of the Service Lifecycle

ITIL V3 approaches service management from the lifecycle aspect of a service. The service lifecycle is an organizational model that provides insight into:
- The way service management is structured.
- The way the various lifecycle components are linked to each other.
- The impact that changes in one component will have on other components and on the entire lifecycle system.

Thus, ITIL V3 focuses on the service lifecycle, and the way service management components are linked. Processes and functions are also discussed in the lifecycle phases.

The service lifecycle consists of five phases. Each volume of the core ITIL books describes one of these phases. The related processes and functions are described in detail in the phase where they have the strongest association.
The five phases are:
1. **Service Strategy** - The phase of strategic planning of service management capabilities, and the alignment of service and business strategies. Processes and functions:
   - Financial management
   - Service portfolio management
   - Demand management
2. **Service Design** - The phase of designing and developing appropriate IT services, including architecture, processes, policy and documents; the design goal is to meet the current and future business requirements. Processes and functions:

- Service catalogue management
- Service level management
- Capacity management
- Availability management
- IT service continuity management
- Information security management
- Supplier management

3. **Service Transition** - The phase of realizing the requirements from previous stages, and improving the capabilities for the transition of new and modified services to production. Processes and functions:
   - Transition planning and support
   - Change management
   - Service asset and configuration management
   - Release and deployment management
   - Service validation and testing
   - Evaluation
   - Knowledge management

4. **Service Operation** - The phase of achieving effectiveness and efficiency in providing and supporting services in order to ensure value for the customer and the service provider. Processes and functions:
   - Event management
   - Incident management
   - Request fulfillment
   - Problem management
   - Access management
   - Monitoring and control
   - IT operations
   - Service desk

5. **Continual Service Improvement** - The phase of creating and maintaining the value for the customer by design improvement, and service introduction and operation. Functions and processes:
   - The 7-step improvement process (CSI Improvement Process)
   - Service reporting

Service Strategy is the axis of the service lifecycle (Figure 2.1) that drives all other phases; it is the phase of policymaking and setting objectives. The Service Design, Service Transition and Service Operation phases are guided by this strategy, their continual theme is adjustment and change. The Continual Service Improvement phase stands for learning and improving, and embraces all other lifecycle phases. This phase initiates

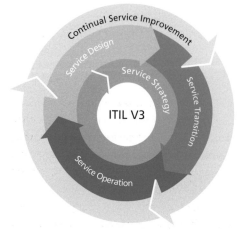

Figure 2.1 The Service Lifecycle (Based on: OGC Source)

improvement programs and projects, and prioritizes them based on the strategic objectives of the organization.

## 2.4 ITIL Library

The ITIL V3 Library encompasses the following components:

- **Core publications** - the five service lifecycle publications:
    - Service Strategy
    - Service Design
    - Service Transition
    - Service Operation
    - Continual Service Improvement

    Each book covers a phase from the service lifecycle and encompasses various processes, functions and activities, which are always described in detail in the book in which they find their key application.

- **Complementary portfolio:**
    - introduction guide
    - key element guides
    - qualification aids
    - white papers
    - glossary

## 2.5 Introduction to Functions and Processes

This section provides an overview of the basic functions and processes that are included in the five phases of the service lifecycle.

Processes and functions are defined as follows:
- **Process** - A structured set of activities designed to accomplish a defined objective. Processes have inputs and outputs, result in a goal-oriented change, and utilize feedback for self-enhancing and self-corrective actions. Processes are **measurable**, provide **results** to **customers** or stakeholders, are continual and iterative and are always **originating from a certain event**. Processes can run through several organizational units. An example of a process is change management.
- **Function** - A team or group of people and the tools they use to carry out one or more processes or activities, specialized in fulfilling a specified type of work, and responsible for specific end results. Functions have their own practices and their own knowledge body. Functions can make use of various processes. An example of a function is a service desk. (Note: "function" can also mean "functionality", "functioning", or "job".)

We can study each process separately to optimize its quality:
- The **process owner** is responsible for the process results.
- The **process manager** is responsible for the realization and structure of the process, and reports to the process owner.
- The **process operatives** are responsible for defined activities, and these activities are reported to the process manager.

The management of the organization can provide control on the basis of data from each process. In most cases, the relevant performance indicators and standards will already be agreed upon, and the process manager can take day-to-day control of the process. The process owner will assess the results based on performance indicators and check whether the results meet the agreed standard. Without clear indicators, it would be difficult for a process owner to determine whether the process is under control, and if planned improvements are being implemented.

Processes are often described using procedures and work instructions:
- A **procedure** is a specified way to carry out an activity or a process. A procedure describes the "how", and can also describe "who" executes the activities. A procedure may include stages from different processes. Procedures will vary depending on the organization.

- A set of **work instructions** defines how one or more activities in a procedure should be executed in detail, using technology or other resources.

When setting up an organization, positions and roles are also used, in addition to the various groups (teams, departments, divisions):
- **Roles** are sets of responsibilities, activities and authorities granted to a person or team. One person or team may have multiple roles; for example, the roles of Configuration Manager and Change Manager may be carried out by one person.
- **Job positions** are traditionally recognized as tasks and responsibilities that are assigned to a specific person. A person in a particular position has a clearly defined package of tasks and responsibilities which may include various roles. Positions can also be more broadly defined as a logical concept that refers to the people and automated measures that carry out a clearly defined process, an activity or a combination of processes or activities. Individuals and roles have an N:N relationship (many-to-many).

People, process, products and partners (the four Ps) provide the main "machinery" of any organization, but they only work well if the machine is oiled: **communication** is an essential element in any organization. If the people do not know about the processes or use the wrong instructions or tools, the outputs may not be as anticipated. Formal structures on communication include:
- **Reporting** - Internal and external reporting, aimed at management or customers, project progress reports, alerts.
- **Meetings** - Formal project meetings, regular meetings with specific targets.
- **Online facilities** - Email systems, chat rooms, pagers, groupware, document sharing systems, messenger facilities, teleconferencing and virtual meeting facilities
- **Notice boards** - Near the coffee maker, at the entrance of the building, in the company restaurant.

It is recommended that a common understanding of processes, projects, programs, and even portfolios is created. The following definitions may be used:
- **Process** - A process is a structured set of activities designed to accomplish a defined objective.
- **Project** - A project is a temporary organization, with people and other assets required to achieve an objective.
- **Program** - A program consists of a number of projects and activities that are planned and managed together to achieve an overall set of related objectives.
- **Portfolio** - A portfolio is a set of projects and/or programs, which are not necessarily related, brought together for the sake of control, coordination and optimization of

the portfolio in its totality. NB: A service portfolio is the complete set of services that are managed by a service provider.

## 2.6 Sample Questions

1. Which of the following does NOT represent a stage in the Service Lifecycle?
   a. Continual Service Improvement
   b. Service Operation
   c. Service Architecture
   d. Service Strategy

2. Which of the following requirements are adequate for an integrated set of Service Management technology?
   1. The tool should have an integrated Configuration Management System to allow the organization's IT infrastructure assets, components and services to be held together with all relevant attributes and to allow relationships between each to be stored and maintained.
   2. The tool should be able to plan changes and assess the impact of changes to minimize the likelihood of post-production problems.
   3. The tool should contain a workflow or process control engine to allow the pre-definition and control of defined processes such as an Incident Lifecycle, Request Fulfilment Lifecycle, Problem Lifecycle, Change Model etc.
   4. The tool should ensure that all of the information within the Service Catalogue is accurate and up to date.
   a. 1 only
   b. 1 and 3 only
   c. 1, 3 and 4 only
   d. All of the above

3. Which of the following should be considered when automating Service Management?
   1. Simplify the service processes before automating them.
   2. Clarify the flow of activities, allocation of tasks, need for information and interactions.
   3. In self service situations, reduce the surface area of the contact users have with the underlying systems and processes.
   4. Do not be in a hurry to automate tasks and interactions that are neither simple nor routine.
   a. 1 only
   b. 1 and 2 only
   c. 1, 2 and 3 only
   d. All of the above

4. Which of the following characterizes a function?
   1. It is specialized to perform a certain type of work.
   2. It is self-contained with capabilities and resources for its performance.
   3. It is responsible for specific outcomes.
   4. It can be repeated and becomes manageable.
   a. 1 only
   b. 1 and 3 only
   c. 1, 2 and 3 only
   d. All of the above

5. Which of the following are characteristics of a process
   1. Measurable
   2. Responds to a specific Event
   3. Has customers
   4. Leads to specific results
   a. 1 only
   b. 1 and 3 only
   c. 1, 2 and 3 only
   d. All of the above

# CHAPTER 3

# Service Strategy

## 3.1 Lifecycle Phase

### 3.1.1 Introduction

In this chapter, the axis (principle line of development, movement, direction, reference point) of the lifecycle is introduced. As the axis of the lifecycle, Service Strategy delivers guidance with designing, developing and implementing service management as a strategic asset. Service Strategy is critical in the context of all processes along the ITIL service lifecycle.

*Goal*

The main **goal** of Service Strategy is to help service providers to develop the ability to think and act in a strategic manner.

*Objectives*

The **objectives** of Service Strategy are to answer questions such as:
- What services to offer to customers?
- How to differentiate from competitors?
- How to create value for customers?
- How to make a case for strategic investments?
- How to define and improve service quality?
- How to efficiently allocate resources across a portfolio of services?

*Scope*

Topics of Service Strategy include:
- strategy generation
- the development of markets (internal and external)
- service assets
- service catalogue
- implementation of strategy through the service lifecycle
- demand management
- financial management
- service portfolio management
- organizational development

- sourcing strategies
- strategic risks

### 3.1.2   Basic concepts

To formulate the strategy, Mintzberg's four Ps are a good starting point (Mintzberg, 1994):
- **Perspective** - Have a clear vision and focus.
- **Position** - Take a clearly defined stance.
- **Plan** - Form a precise notion of how the organization should develop itself.
- **Pattern** - Maintain consistency in decisions and actions.

**Value creation** is a combination of the effects of utility and warranty. Both are necessary for the creation of value for the customer. For customers, the positive effect is the "utility" of a service; the insurance of this positive effect is the "warranty":
- **Utility - fitness for purpose**. Functionality offered by a product or service to meet a particular need. Utility is often summarized as "what it does".
- **Warranty - fitness for use**. A promise or guarantee that a product or service will meet its agreed requirements. The availability, capacity, continuity and information security necessary to meet the customers' requirements.

The **value networks** are defined as follows: "A value network is a web of relationships that generate both tangible and intangible value through complex and dynamic exchanges between two or more organizations."

Resources and capabilities are the **service assets** of a service provider. Organizations use them to create value in the form of goods and services.
- **Resources** - Resources include IT Infrastructure, people, money or anything else that might help to deliver an IT service. Resources are considered to be the assets of an organization.
- **Capabilities** - Capabilities develop over the years. Service providers must develop distinctive capabilities in order to maintain services that are difficult to duplicate by the competition. Service providers must also invest substantially in education and training if they are to continue to develop their strategic assets and maintain their competitive advantage.

Service providers are organizations that supply services to one or more internal or external customers. Three different types of service providers are distinguished:
- **Type I: Internal service provider** - An internal service provider that is embedded within a Business Unit. There may be several type I service providers within an organization.
- **Type II: Shared Services Unit** - An internal service provider that provides shared IT services to more than one Business Unit.
- **Type III: External service provider** - A service provider that provides IT services to external customers.

The **service portfolio** represents the opportunities and readiness of a service provider to serve the customers and the market space. The service portfolio can be divided into three subsets of services:
- **Service catalogue** - The services that are available to customers.
- **Service pipeline** - The services that are either under consideration or in development.
- **Retired services** - Services that are phased out or withdrawn.

### 3.1.3  Processes and other activities
This section briefly explains the processes and activities of Service Strategy.
More information about each of these processes can be found in 3.2 of this pocket guide.

The Service Strategy processes:
- **Financial management** - An integral component of service management. It anticipates the essential management information in financial terms that is required for the guarantee of efficient and cost-effective service delivery.
- **Demand management** - An essential aspect of service management in which offer and demand are harmonized. The goal of demand management is to predict, as accurately as possible, the purchase of products and, where possible, to balance the demand with the resources.
- **Service Portfolio Management (SPM)** - Method to manage all service management investments in terms of business value. The objective of SPM is to achieve maximum value creation while at the same time managing the risks and costs.

The Service Strategy activities:
- **Defining the market** - Understand the relation between services and strategies, understand the customers, understand the opportunities, and classify and visualize the services.

- **The development of the offer** - Create a service portfolio that represents the opportunities and readiness of a service provider to serve the customers and the market.
- **The development of strategic assets** - Define the value network and improve capabilities and resources (service assets) to increase the service and performance potential.
- **Preparation for execution** - Strategic assessment, setting objectives, defining critical success factors, prioritizing investments, et cetera.

### 3.1.4 Organization
There are five recognizable phases in organizational development within the spectrum of centralization and decentralization:
1. **Stage 1: Network** - An organization in stage 1 focuses on fast, informal and ad hoc provision of services. The organization is technologically oriented and is uncomfortable with formal structures.
2. **Stage 2: Directive** - In stage 2, the informal structure of stage 1 is transformed into an hierarchical structure with a strong management team. They assume the responsibility for leading the strategy and for guiding managers to embrace their functional responsibilities.
3. **Stage 3: Delegation** - In stage 3, efforts are made to enhance technical efficiency and provide space for innovation in order to reduce costs and improve services.
4. **Stage 4: Coordination** - In stage 4 the focus is directed towards the use of formal systems as a means of achieving better coordination.
5. **Stage 5: Collaboration** - During stage 5, the focus is on the improvement of cooperation with the business.

The goal of the Service Strategy phase is to improve the core competencies. Sometimes it is more efficient to outsource certain services. We call this the SOC principle (Separation of Concerns, SOC): that which results from the search for competitive differentiation through the redistribution of resources and capabilities.
The following generic forms of outsourcing can be delineated:
- **Internal outsourcing**:
  - Type 1 Internal - Provision and delivery of services by internal staff; this offers the most control, but is limited in scale.
  - Type 2 Shared services - Working with internal BUs; offers lower costs than Type 1 and more standardization, but is still limited in scale.
- **Traditional outsourcing**:
  - Complete outsourcing of a service - A single contract with one service provider; better in terms of scaling opportunities, but limited in best-in-class capabilities.

- **Multi-vendor outsourcing**:
  - **Prime** - A single contract with one service provider who works with multiple providers; improved capabilities and risks, but increased complexity.
  - **Consortium** - A selection of multiple service providers; the advantage is best-in-class with more oversight; the disadvantage is the risk of the necessity of working with the competition.
  - **Selective outsourcing** - A pool of service providers selected and managed through the service receiver; this is the most difficult structure to manage.
  - **Co-Sourcing** - A variation of selective outsourcing in which the service receiver combines a structure of internal or shared services with external providers; in this case, the service receiver is the service integrator.

*Roles and responsibilities*

Important roles and responsibilities are:
- **Chief sourcing officer** - The chief sourcing officer reports to the CIO and manages the implementation of sourcing.
- **Director of service management** - The director supervises the provider on behalf of the business.
- **Contract manager** - The contract manager manages the service contract from the perspective of the service provider.
- **Product manager** - The product manager is a key role within service portfolio management. The role is responsible for managing the services in the service provider's organization. Works closely with the business relationship manager.
- **Business relationship manager** - The business relationship manager brings coordination and focus to the customer portfolio. This role represents the customer.
- **Process owner** - The process owner manages the process models that have been developed on behalf of the users.
- **Business representatives** - They represent the customers' interests and manage the sourcing relationship from that perspective.
- The **financial manager** - The financial manager is responsible for implementing and managing the IT Service providers budgeting, accounting and charging.

### 3.1.5 Methods, techniques and tools

Services are socio-technical systems with service assets as the operational elements. The effectiveness of Service Strategy depends on a well-managed relationship between the social and technical sub-systems. It is essential to identify and manage these dependencies and influences.

Tools for the Service Strategy phase can be:
- **Simulation** - System Dynamics is a methodology for understanding and managing the complex problems of IT organizations.
- **Analytical modeling** - Six Sigma, PMBOK® and PRINCE2® offer well tested methods based on analytical models. They must be evaluated and adopted within the context of Service Strategy and service management.

Three techniques for quantifying the value of an investment are suggested:
- **Business case** - A way of identifying business objectives that are dependent on service management.
- **Pre-Program ROI** - Techniques used to quantitatively analyze investments before committing resources.
- **Post-Program ROI** - Techniques used to retroactively analyze investments.

### 3.1.6   Implementation and operation

Strategic goals are to be converted into plans with objectives and ultimate goals, based on the lifecycle. Plans translate the intentions of the strategy into actions, through Service Design, Service Transition, Service Operation, and Continual Service Improvement.

Service Strategy provides every phase of the lifecycle with input:
- **Strategy and design** - Service strategies are implemented through the delivery of the portfolio in a specific market area. Newly chartered services or services that require improvements in order to suit the demand are promoted to the Service Design phase. The design can be driven by service models, outcomes, constraints or pricing.
- **Strategy and transition** - To reduce the risk of failing, all strategic changes go through Service Transition. Service Transition processes analyze, evaluate and approve strategic initiatives. Service Strategy provides Service Transition with structures and constraints like the service portfolio, policies, architectures, and the contract portfolio.
- **Strategy and operations** - The final realization of strategy occurs in the production phase. The strategy must be in line with operational capabilities and constraints. Deployment patterns in Service Operation define operational strategies for customers. Service Operation is responsible for delivering the contract portfolio and should be able to deal with demand changes.
- **Strategy and CSI** - Due to constant changes, strategies are never static. Service strategies need to be developed, adopted and continually reviewed. Strategic imperatives influence quality perspectives processed in CSI. CSI processes deliver

feedback for the strategy phase on, for example: quality perspective, warranty factors, reliability, maintainability, redundancy.

Challenges and opportunities:
- **Complexity** - IT organizations are complex systems. This explains why some service organizations are not inclined to change. Organizations are not always in a position to anticipate the long-term consequences of decisions and actions. Without continual learning processes, today's decisions often end up as tomorrow's problems.
- **Coordination and control** - The people who make the decisions often have limited time, attention and capacity. Therefore they delegate the roles and responsibilities to teams and individuals. This makes coordination through cooperation and monitoring essential.
- **Preserving Value** - Customers are not only interested in the utility and warranty that they receive for the price they pay. They want to know the Total Cost of Utilization (TCU).
- **Effectiveness in measurement** - Measurements focus the organization on its strategic goals, follow the progression and provide the organization with feedback. Most IT organizations are good at monitoring data, but often they are not very good at providing insights into the effectiveness of the services that they offer. It is crucial to perform the right analyses and to modify them as the strategy changes.

The implementation of strategy leads to changes in the service portfolio. This involves management of related risks. Risk is defined as follows: *"a risk is an uncertain outcome, or in other words, a positive opportunity or a negative threat."* Risk analysis and risk management must be applied to the service pipeline and service catalogue in order to identify, curb and mitigate the risks within the lifecycle phases.

The following types of risks are recognized:
- contract risks
- design risks
- operational risks
- market risks

## 3.2   Functions and Processes

### 3.2.1   Financial Management

*Introduction*
Financial management is an integrated component of service management. It provides vital information that management needs to guarantee efficient and cost-effective service delivery. If strictly implemented, financial management generates meaningful and critical data on performance. It is also able to answer important organizational issues, such as:
- Does our differentiation strategy result in higher profits and revenue, reduced costs or increased coverage?
- Which services cost most and why?
- Where are our greatest inefficiencies?

Financial management ensures that the charges for IT services are transparent via the service catalogue and that the business understands them. The benefits are:
- improved decision-making
- inputs for service portfolio management
- financial compliance and control
- operational control
- value capture and creation

*Basic concepts*
Two vital value concepts for service valuation are defined:
- **Provisioning value** - The actual underlying costs of IT (creation costs), both tangible and intangible. Examples of these costs include: hardware and software license costs, annual maintenance costs, facility costs, taxes, compliance costs.
- **Service value potential** - The value-adding component based on the customer's value perception or the expected additional utility and warranty that the customers can obtain compared to their own assets. Looks at the service's individual value components to determine the true value of the service. Determines the eventual value of the service by adding these components and comparing them against the costs (provisioning value).

Financial Management ensures correct funding for the purchase and the delivery of services. The expected demand for IT services is qualified and translated into financial terms via a plan. This plan may have three primary areas, each of which delivers financial results that are necessary for continued transparency and service valuation:

- **Operating and capital planning** (general and fixed asset ledgers) - Translation of IT expenditures to collective financial systems as part of the collective planning cycle.
- **Demand planning** - Need for and use of IT services as described earlier.
- **Regulatory and environmental planning** (compliance) - driven from the business.

Financial management acts as a bridge between financial systems and service management systems. A service-oriented accounting function results in far more detail and understanding of the delivery and consumption of services, as well as the production of data for the planning process. Related functions and accounting properties are:

- **Service recording** - Allocating a cost center for a service.
- **Cost types** - High-level expenses, such as hardware, software, personnel costs, administration.
    - Once the basis for cost administration (e.g. per department, service or customer) is established, cost types are determined for cost entry.
    - The number of cost types can vary depending on the organization's size.
    - Cost types must have a clear and recognizable description, so that costs can be easily allocated.
    - The cost types can then be split up into cost items and settlement for each cost item may be established at a later stage.
- **Cost classification** - To ensure good cost control, it is important to gain insight into the types of costs that occur. Costs can be split up according to various aspects.

**Variable Cost Dynamics** (**VCD**) analyzes and searches for insight into the many variables that have an impact on the service costs. The VCD analysis is able to determine the expected impact of events like acquisitions, divestments and changes in the service portfolio or service alternatives.

*Activities*
During service valuation activities, the following decisions are made:

- **Direct costs versus indirect costs** - Can costs be attributed directly to a specific service or are they shared by several services (indirect costs)? Once the depth and width of the cost components have been identified, rules or policy plans may be required to indicate how the costs must be spread across the services.
- **Labor costs** - Develop a system to calculate the wage costs for a certain service.
- **Variable costs** - Variable expenses that depend on e.g. the number of users or the number of occurring events. To predict variable costs, you can use:
    - <u>Tiers</u> - Identify price breaks to encourage customers to buy a specific volume that is efficient to the customer and provider.

- – Maximum costs - Describe the costs of a service based on maximum variation.
- – Average costs - Set the costs at an average calculated over a defined period.
- **Translation of cost account data to service value** - Can be done only if the costs are linked to services.

After having established the fixed and variable costs for each service, the variable cost drivers and variation level of a service should be determined.

Traditional models to fund IT services include:
- **Rolling plan funding** - A constant funding cycle; suitable for a service lifecycle for which a funding obligation is incurred at the start of a cycle and continues until changes occur or the cycle ends.
- **Trigger based plans** - Critical triggers activate planning for a specific event; the change management process, for instance, could act as a trigger for the planning process for all approved changes that have financial consequences.
- **Zero based funding** - Only include the actual costs of a service.

The **Business Impact Analysis** (BIA) represents the basis for planning business continuity. BIA identifies the financial and operational impact that may result from an interruption of business operations as well as the impact on assets and customers. This information can help shape and improve operational performance. This is because it enables improved decision-making with regard to prioritization of incident handling, the focus of problem management, change management, release and deployment management, and project prioritization. BIA offers an additional tool to determine the costs of service failure and the relative value of a service. The costs of a service failure consist of the value of lost productivity and income for a specific period.

Some concepts in financial management have a big impact on the development of service strategies. A number of these are highlighted, allowing each organization to determine which the best alternatives are for its Service Strategy:
- **Cost Recovery, Value Center, or Accounting Center?** - IT's financial cycle starts with investment in resources that create the outputs. Customers identify those outputs as value, reinitiating the cycle. Depending on the acknowledgement of the added value, IT is then considered a cost center or a valuable asset for the business objectives.
- **Chargeback: to charge or not to charge?** - A chargeback model for IT can enable justification and transparency. Charging increases the customer organization's awareness of the costs incurred to provide it with information.

There are several chargeback models:
- **Notional charging** - An accounting method that provides insight into the costs that would be charged for a specific settlement method.
- **Metered usage** - Settling costs on the basis of carefully established consumption units; applies exclusively for organizations that have made serious progress in introducing financial management.
- **Direct plus** - Less complex settlement model in which the allocated direct costs of a service are increased by a percentage of the general indirect costs for shared services.
- **Fixed or user cost** - Simplest settlement model in which the costs are divided on the basis of an accepted computing factor, such as the number of users; this method does not allow for much distinction and therefore makes the least contribution to cost awareness.
- **Financial Management implementation checklist** - A number of example implementation steps for phased implementation: plan, analyze, design, implement, measure.

*Inputs and outputs*
Financial Management gathers data inputs from the whole organization and helps to generate and disseminate information as an output to base critical decisions and activities on.

### 3.2.2 Service Portfolio Management

*Introduction*

A **service portfolio** describes the services of a provider in terms of business value. It is a dynamic method used to govern investments in service management across the enterprise, in terms of financial values. With Service Portfolio Management (SPM), managers are able to assess the quality requirements and accompanying costs.

The **goal** of service portfolio management is to realize maximum value while managing risks and costs.

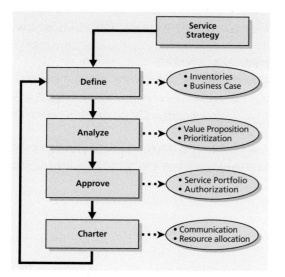

Figure 3.1 Service portfolio management (Based on: OGC Source)

*Basic concepts*

By functioning as the basis of the decision framework, the service portfolio helps to answer the following strategic questions:
- Why should a client buy these services?
- Why should a client buy these services from us?
- What are the price and charge back models?
- What are our strong and weak points, our priorities and our risks?
- How should our resources and capabilities be allocated?

With an efficient portfolio having optimal ROI and risk levels, an organization can maximize the value realization on its constrained and limited resources and capabilities.

Product managers play an important role in the service portfolio management. They are responsible for managing services as products during the entire lifecycle. Product managers coordinate and focus the organization and own the service catalogue. They work closely together with the Business Relationship Managers, who coordinate and focus on the Client Portfolio. In essence, SPM is a Governance method.

The service portfolio covers three subsets of services:
- **Service catalogue** - That part of the service portfolio that is visible to customers. The service catalogue is an essential strategy tool because it can be viewed as the virtual projection of the actual and available capabilities of the service provider.
- **Service pipeline** - Consists of all services that are either under consideration or in development for a specific market or customer. These services are to be applied in the production phase via the Service Transition phase. The pipeline represents the growth and strategic anticipation for the future.
- **Retired services** - Services that are phased out or withdrawn. The phasing out of services is a component of Service Transition and is necessary to guarantee that all agreements with customers will be kept.

*Activities*
SPM is a dynamic and continuous process that entails the following work methods (see also Figure 3.1):
- **Define** - Making an inventory of services, business cases and validating the portfolio data; start with collecting information on all existing and proposed services in order to determine the costs of the existing portfolio; the cyclic nature of the SPM process signifies that this phase does not only inventory the services, but also validates the data over and over again; each service in the portfolio should have a business case.
- **Analyze** - Maximizing the portfolio value, tuning, prioritizing and balancing supply and demand; in this phase, the strategic goals are given a concrete form. Start with a series of top/down questions such as: What are the long-term goals of the service organization? Which services are required to realize these goals? Which capabilities and resources are necessary to attain these services? The answers to these questions form the basis of the analysis, but also determine the desired result of SPM. Service investments must be subdivided into three strategic categories:
  - **Run the Business** - RTB investments concentrate on maintaining the service production.

- **Grow the Business** - GTB investments are intended to expand the scope of services.
- **Transform the Business** - TTB investments are meant to move into new market spaces.
- **Approve** - Finishing the proposed portfolio, authorizing services and resources and making decisions for the future. There are six different outcomes: retain, replace, rationalize, re-factor, renew and retire.
- **Charter** - Communicating decisions, allocating resources and chartering services. Start with a list of decisions and action items and communicate these clearly and unambiguously to the organization. Decisions must be in tune with the budget decisions and financial plans. New services proceed to the Services Design Phase and existing services are renewed in the service catalogue.

### Inputs and outputs

Financial management is a key input to service portfolio management. By understanding cost structures applied in the provisioning of a service, service costs can be benchmarked against other providers. This IT financial information can be used together with service demand and internal capability information. This way, beneficial decisions can be made regarding whether a certain service should be provisioned internally (the output).

Service portfolio management provides input for refreshing services in the service catalogue.

### 3.2.3 Demand Management

*Introduction*
Demand management is a vital aspect of service management. It aligns supply with demand and aims to predict the sale of products as closely as possible and, if possible, even regulate it.

Service management must deal with the additional problem of synchronous production and consumption. Service Operation is impossible without the existence of a demand that consumes the product. It is a pull-system, in which consumption cycles stimulate the production cycles (Figure 3.2).

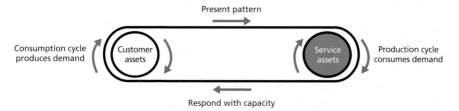

Figure 3.2 Close relationship between demand and capacity (Based on: OGC Source)

It is not possible to produce service output and store it until demand arises. The production capacity of the resources available for a service is therefore adjusted in accordance with demand prognoses and patterns.

**Activity-based demand management**: business processes are the primary source of demand for services. **Patterns of Business Activity (PBA)** have an impact on demand patterns seen by the service providers.

It is extremely important to study the customer's business and thus identify, analyze and record patterns. This creates sufficient basis for capacity mananagement.

A **user profile (UP)** is a pattern of user demand for IT services. They are based on roles and responsibilities within organizations for people, and functions and operations for processes and applications. Each user profile can be associated with one or more Patterns of Business Activity.

*Basic concepts*
- **Service packages** - A service package is a detailed description of an IT service that can be delivered to customers. A service package consists of a Service Level Package (SLP) and one or more core services and supporting services.
- **Service Level Package (SLP)** - A defined level of utility and warranty for a particular service package, from the perspective of the user. Each SLP is designed to meet the needs of a particular Pattern of Business Activity (PBA).
- **Core Service Package (CSP)** - A detailed description of a core service that may be shared by two or more service level packages.
- **Line of Service (LOS)** - A core service or supporting service that has multiple service level packages. A line of service is managed by a product manager and each service level package is designed to support a particular market segment.

*Activities*
**Core services** deliver the basic results to the customer. They represent the value that customers require and for which they are willing to pay. Core services represent the basis for the value-proposition to the customer. Supporting services enable that value proposition (enabling services or Basic Factors) or improve it (Enhancing services or Excitement Factors).

Bundling core services and supporting services are a vital aspect of a market strategy. Service providers should thoroughly analyze the prevailing conditions in their business environment, the needs of the customer segments or types they serve, and the alternatives that are available to these customers. These are strategic decisions - they shape a long-term vision that is intended to enable the organization to create lasting value for customers, even if the methods, standards, technologies and regulations in an industry change. Bundling supporting services with core services affects Service Operations and represents challenges for the Design, Transition and CSI (Continual Service Improvement) phases.

Service providers must focus on the effective delivery of value through core services, while at the same time keeping an eye on the supporting services. Research has shown that customers are often dissatisfied with supporting services. Some supporting services, such as the helpdesk or technical support, are generally bundled but can also be offered separately. This is an important consideration in the strategic planning and review of the plans. These strategic decisions can have a major impact on the service provider's success at the portfolio level. They are important primarily to service providers who supply multiple organizations or business units while at the same time being forced to reduce costs in order to preserve the competitiveness of their portfolio.

*Inputs and outputs*

Business processes are the primary inputs for demand management. Patterns of Business Activity (PBAs) influence the demand forecasts and patterns. Analyzing PBAs within demand management can deliver inputs to other service management processes such as:

- Service Design - To make the design suit the demand patterns.
- Service catalogue management - To have the appropriate services available.
- Service portfolio management - To approve investing in additional capacity, new services, changes to services.
- Financial management - To approve suitable incentives to influence demand.

Inputs:
- resource utilization profiles of services
- PBAs

Outputs:
- financial constraints (e.g. pricing and charging policies)
- physical constraints (e.g. limited availability)

## 3.3  Sample Questions

1. A risk is measured by:
   1. the probability of a threat
   2. the vulnerability of the asset to a threat
   3. the countermeasures put in place
   4. the impact if a threat occurs
   a. 1 only
   b. 2 and 4 only
   c. 1, 2 and 4 only
   d. All of the above

2. The value of a service is determined by:
   1. Preferences
   2. Practice
   3. Perceptions
   4. Business outcome
   a. 1 only
   b. 1 and 3 only
   c. 1, 3 and 4 only
   d. All of the above

3.  What are the MAIN activities in the Service Strategy management process?
    1.  Define the market
    2.  Develop the offerings
    3.  Develop strategic assets
    4.  Prepare for execution
    a.  4 only
    b.  2 and 3 only
    c.  1, 2 and 3 only
    d.  All of the above

4.  Which of the following activities is NOT an activity in the Financial Management process?
    a.  Service devaluation
    b.  Service Portfolio Management
    c.  Service Investment Analysis
    d.  Compliance

5.  Which of the following concepts and activities help Demand Management in managing the demand for services?
    1.  Differentiated offerings
    2.  Differentiated service levels
    3.  Major Incident Management
    4.  Analysing and tracking the activity patterns of a business process
    a.  4 only
    b.  1 and 2 only
    c.  1, 2 and 4 only
    d.  All of the above

CHAPTER 4

# Service Design

## 4.1  Lifecycle Phase

### 4.1.1  Introduction

*Goal*
Service Design deals with the design and development of services and their related processes. The main **goal** of Service Design is: the design of new or changed services for introduction into a production environment.

*Objectives*
The **Objectives** of Service Design include:
*   contribute to the business objectives
*   where possible, contribute to saving time and money
*   minimize or prevent risks
*   contribute to satisfying the current and future market needs
*   assess and improve the effectiveness and efficiency of IT services
*   support the development of policies and standards regarding IT services
*   contribute to the quality of IT services

The Service Design phase in the lifecycle begins with the demand for new or changed requirements from the customer. Good preparation and an effective and efficient infusion of people, processes, products (services, technology and tools) and partners (suppliers, manufacturers and vendors) - ITIL's four Ps - are a must if the design, plans and projects are to succeed.

*Value for the business*
Good Service Design offers the following benefits:
*   lower Total Cost of Ownership (TCO)
*   improved quality of service delivery
*   improved consistency of the service
*   simpler implementation of new or modified services
*   improved synchronization of services with the needs of the business
*   improved effectiveness of performances

- improved IT administration
- more effective service management and IT processes
- more simplified decision-making

### 4.1.2   Basic concepts

*Scope*
The design phase should cover five major aspects:
1.  **The design of service solutions** - A structured design approach is necessary in order to produce a new service for the right costs, functionality, and quality, including all of the functional requirements, resources and capabilities needed and agreed. The process must be iterative and incremental in order to satisfy the customers' changing wishes and requirements. It is important to assemble a Service Design Package (SDP) with all aspects of the (new or changed) service and its requirements through each stage of its lifecycle.
2.  **The design of the service portfolio** - The service portfolio is the most critical management system for supporting all of the processes. It describes the service delivery in terms of value for the customer and must include all of the service information and its status. In any event, the portfolio makes clear in which phase the service takes place; from defining the requirements until retiring of the service.
3.  **The design of the architecture** - The activities include preparing the blueprints for the development and deployment of an IT infrastructure, the applications, the data and the environment (according to the needs of the business). This architecture design is defined as: "the development and maintenance of IT policies, strategies, architectures, designs, documents, plans and processes for deployment, implementation and improvement of appropriate IT services and solutions throughout the organization."
4.  **The design of processes** - A **process model** enables understanding and helps to articulate the distinctive features of a process. By defining what the activities in the lifecycle phases are and what the inputs and outputs are, it is possible to work more efficiently and effectively, and in a more customer-oriented way. By assessing the current quality of processes and the options for improvement, the organization can enhance its efficiency and effectiveness even further. The next step is to establish norms and standards. This way the organization can link the quality requirements with the outputs. This approach corresponds with Deming's **Plan-Do-Check-Act** Management Cycle.
5.  **The design of measurement systems and metrics** - In order to lead and manage the development process of services effectively, regular assessments of service quality must be performed. The selected assessment system must be synchronized with the

capacity and maturity of the processes that are assessed. There are four elements that can be investigated: **progress, fulfillment, effectiveness** and **efficiency of the process**.

The question which model should be used for the development of IT services largely depends on the **service delivery model** that is chosen. The delivery options are:

- **Insourcing** - Internal resources are used for the design, development, maintenance, execution, and/or support for the service.
- **Outsourcing** - Engaging an external organization for the design, development, maintenance, execution, and/or support of the service.
- **Co-sourcing** - A combination of insourcing and outsourcing in which various outsourcing organizations work cooperatively throughout the service lifecycle.
- **Multi-sourcing** (or partnership) - Multiple organizations make formal agreements with the focus on strategic partnerships (creating new market opportunities).
- **Business Process Outsourcing (BPO)** - An external organization provides and manages (part of) another organization's business processes in another location.
- **Application service provision** - Computer-based services are offered to the customer over a network.
- **Knowledge Process Outsourcing (KPO)** - Provides domain-based processes and business expertise.

Traditional **development approaches** are based on the principle that the requirements of the customer can be determined at the beginning of the service lifecycle and that the development costs can be kept under control by managing the changes. Rapid Application Development (RAD) approaches begin with the notion that change is inevitable and that discouraging change simply indicates passivity in regard to the market. The RAD-approach is an incremental and iterative development approach:

- **The incremental approach** - A service is designed bit by bit. Parts are developed separately and are delivered individually. Each piece supports one of the business functions that the entire service needs. The big advantage in this approach is its shorter delivery time. The development of each part, however, requires that all phases of the lifecycle are traversal.
- **The iterative approach** - The development lifecycle is repeated several times. Techniques like prototyping are used in order to understand the customer-specific requirements better.

A combination of the two approaches is possible. An organization can begin by specifying the requirements for the entire service, followed by an incremental design and the development of the software. Many organizations however, choose standard software solutions to satisfy needs and demands instead of designing the service themselves.

### 4.1.3   Processes and other activities
This section briefly explains the processes and activities of the Service Design. More information about each of these processes can be found in 4.2 of this study guide.

Service Design processes:
- **Service Catalogue Management (SCM)** - The goal of SCM is the development and maintenance of a service catalogue that includes all of the accurate details and the status of all operational services and those being prepared to run operationally, and the business processes they support.
- **Service Level Management (SLM)** - The goal of SLM is to ensure that the levels of IT service delivery are documented, agreed and achieved, for both existing services and future services in accordance with the agreed targets.
- **Capacity management** - The goal of capacity management is to ensure that the capacity corresponds to both the existing and future needs of the customer (recorded in a capacity plan).
- **Availability management** - The goal of the availability management process is to ensure that the availability level of both new and changed services corresponds with the levels as agreed with the customer. It must maintain in an Availability Management Information System (AMIS) which forms the basis the availability plan.
- **IT Service Continuity Management (ITSCM)** - The ultimate goal of ITSCM is to support business continuity (vital business functions, VBF) by ensuring that the required IT facilities can be restored within the agreed time.
- **Information security management** - Information security management ensures that the information security policy satisfies the organization's overall security policy and the requirements originating from corporate governance.
- **Supplier management** - Supplier management draws attention to all of the suppliers and contracts in order to support the delivery of services to the customer.

Service Design technology-related activities:
- **Development of requirements** - Understanding and documenting the business and user's requirements (functional requirements, management and operational requirements and usability requirements).
- **Data and information management** - Data is one of the most critical matters that must be kept under control in order to develop, deliver and support effective IT services.

- **Application management** - Applications, along with data and infrastructure, comprise the technical components of IT services.

### 4.1.4   Organization

Well performing organizations can quickly and accurately make the right decisions and execute them successfully. In order to achieve this, it is crucial that the roles and responsibilities are clearly defined. This is also an essential issue in the Service Design phase. One of the possible models that can be helpful in this regard is the **RACI model**. RACI is an acronym for the four most important roles:

- Responsible - the person who is responsible for completing the task
- Accountable - just one person who is accountable for each task
- Consulted - people who give advice
- Informed - people who must be kept in the loop regarding the progress of the project

In establishing a RACI system, the following steps are required:

- identify activities and processes
- identify and define functional roles
- conduct meetings and delegate the RACI-codes
- identify gaps and potential overlaps
- distribute the chart and build in feedback
- ensure that the allocations are followed

|            | Role 1 | Role 2 | Role 3 | Role 4 |
|------------|--------|--------|--------|--------|
| Activity 1 | R      | A      | I      | C      |
| Activity 2 | I      | C      | R      | A      |
| Activity 3 | R      | A      | I      | C      |
| Activity 4 | I      | A      | C      | R      |

Table 4.1 Structure of a RACI matrix

The most important roles of Service Design are:

- **The process owner** is responsible for ensuring that the process is implemented as agreed and that the established objectives will therefore be achieved. Tasks are:
  - documenting and recording the process
  - defining the KPIs and if necessary revising them
  - improving the effectiveness and efficiency of the process
  - providing input to the Service Improvement Plan
  - reviewing the process, the roles and responsibilities

- **The service design manager** is responsible for the overall coordination and inputting of the service designs. Tasks include:
  - ensure that the overall service strategies are reflected in the Service Design practice and that the designs meet the business requirements
  - design the functional aspects of the services
  - produce and maintain the design documentation
  - assess the effectiveness and efficiency of Service Design
- **The service catalogue manager** is responsible for the production and maintenance of the service catalogue. In addition, the service catalogue manager must:
  - ensure that the services are recorded in the service catalogue
  - ensure that the information that has been included is up-to-date and is consistent with the information in the service portfolio
  - ensure that the service catalogue is secure and that there are backups
- **The service level manager** responsibilities include:
  - have an insight into the changing demands of the customer and the market
  - ensure that the customers' existing and future requirements have been identified
  - negotiate and make agreements on the delivery of services
  - assist in the production and maintenance of an accurate service portfolio
  - ensure that the objectives that have been ratified in underlying contracts are synchronized with the SLA
- **The availability manager's** responsibilities include:
  - ensure that the existing services are available as agreed
  - assist in investigating and diagnosing all incidents and problems
  - contribute to the design of the IT infrastructure
  - proactively improve the availability of services
- **The security manager's** responsibilities include:
  - design and maintain the information security policy
  - communicate with the involved parties on matters pertaining to the security policy
  - assist in the business impact analysis
  - perform risk analyses and risk management together with availability management and IT service continuity management
- The **IT service continuity manager's** responsibilities include:
  - perform business impact analyses
  - implement and maintain the ITSCM process in accordance with overall requirements
  - ensure that ITSCM plans, risks and activities align with those of BCM
  - maintain and develop the continuity strategy
  - undertake reviews of the continuity plans

- The **capacity manager's** responsibilities include:
  - ensure there is adequate IT capacity to meet required levels of service
  - identify capacity requirements
  - understand current usage
  - perform sizing on all proposed new services
  - forecast future capacity requirements
- The **supplier manager's** responsibilities include:
  - provide assistance with SLAs, contracts and agreements for third-party suppliers
  - ensure value for money is obtained from all suppliers
  - review and maintain Supplier and contract database
  - monitor and report supplier performance
  - coordinate and support all IT supplier and contract managers

Additional roles that can be found in this phase include:
- IT planner
- IT designer/architect

### 4.1.5  Methods, techniques and tools
It is extremely important to ensure that the tools to be used support the processes and not the other way around. There are various tools and techniques that can be used for supporting the service and component designs. Not only do they make the hardware and software designs possible, but they also enable the development of environment designs, process designs and data designs. Tools help ensure that Service Design processes function effectively. They enhance efficiency and provide valuable management information on the identification of possible weak points.

### 4.1.6  Implementation and operation
In the following section the implementation considerations for Service Design are addressed.
- **Business Impact Analysis (BIA)** - BIA is a valuable source of information for establishing the customer's needs, and the impact and risk of a service (for the business). The BIA is an essential element in the business continuity process and dictates the strategy to be followed for risk reduction and recovery after a catastrophe.
- **Implementation of Service Design** - Process, policy and architecture for the design of IT services, must be documented and used in order to design and implement appropriate IT services. In principle, they all should be implemented because all processes are related and often depend on each other. In this way you will get the best benefit. It is important do this in a structured way.

- **Prerequisites for Success (PFS)** - Prerequisites are often requirements from other processes. For example, before Service Level Management (SLM) can design the Service Level Agreement (SLA), a Business service catalogue and a Technical service catalogue are necessary.

KPIs for the Service Design process include:
- Accuracy of the SLAs, OLAs and UCs.
- Percentage of specifications of the requirements of Service Design produced within budget.
- Percentage of Service Design Packages (SDPs) produced on time.

Examples of challenges that are faced during implementation include:
- The need for synchronization of existing architecture, strategy and policy.
- The use of diverse technologies and applications instead of single platforms.
- Unclear or changing customer requirements.

There are several risks during the Service Design phase, including:
- Maturity - if the maturity of one process is low, it is impossible to reach a high level of maturity in other processes.
- Unclear Business requirements.
- Too little time allotted for Service Design.

Figure 4.1 shows that the output from every phase becomes an input to another phase in the lifecycle. Thus Service Strategy provides important input to Service Design, which in turn, provides input to the transition phase. The service portfolio provides information to every process in every phase of the lifecycle.

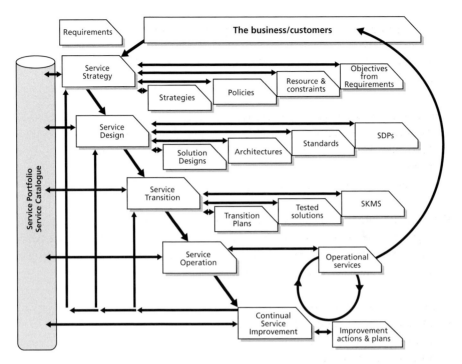

Figure 4.1 The most important relationships, inputs and outputs of Service Design (Based on: OGC Source)

## 4.2 Functions and Processes

### 4.2.1 Service Catalogue Management

*Introduction*
The purpose of Service Catalogue Management (SCM) is the development and upkeep of a service catalogue that contains all details, status, possible interactions and mutual dependencies of all present services and those under development.

*Basic concepts*
Over years, an organization's IT infrastructure grows at a steady pace. For this reason, it is difficult to obtain an accurate picture of the services offered by the organization and who they are offered to. To get a clearer picture, a service portfolio is developed (with a service catalogue as part of it), and kept up-to-date. The development of the service portfolio is a component of the Service Strategy phase.

It is important to make a clear distinction between the service portfolio and the service catalogue:
- **Service portfolio** - The service portfolio contains information about each service and its status. As a result, the portfolio describes the entire process, starting with the client requirements for the development, building and execution of the service. The service portfolio represents all active and inactive services in the various phases of the lifecycle.
- **Service catalogue** - The service catalogue is a subset of the service portfolio and only consists of active and approved services (at user level) in Service Operation. The service catalogue divides services into components. It contains policies, guidelines and responsibilities, as well as prices, service level agreements and delivery conditions.

Many organizations integrate and maintain the service portfolio and service catalogue as a part of their Configuration Management System (CMS). By defining every service the organization can relate the incidents and Requests for Change to the services in question. Therefore changes in both service portfolio and service catalogue must be included in the change management process.

The service catalogue can also be used for a Business Impact Analysis (BIA) as part of IT Service Continuity Management (ITSCM), or as starting point for the re-distribution of the workload as part of capacity management. These benefits justify the investment (in time and money) involved in preparing a catalogue and making it worthwhile.

The **service catalogue** has two aspects:
- **Business service catalogue** - Contains all details of the services that are being supplied to the client, and the relations with different departments and processes that depend on the service.
- **Technical service catalogue** - Contains not only the details of the services supplied to the client, but also their relation to the supporting and shared services, components and CIs. This is *the part that is not visible to* the client.

A combination of both aspects provides a quick overview on the impact of incidents and changes. For this reason, many mature organizations combine both aspects in a service catalogue, as part of a service portfolio.

*Activities*
The service catalogue is the only resource which contains consistent information about all services of the service provider. The catalogue should be accessible to every authorized person. Activities include:
- Defining the services.
- Producing and maintaining an accurate service catalogue.
- Providing information about the service catalogue to stakeholders.
- Managing the interaction, mutual dependency, consistency and monitoring of the service portfolio.
- Managing the interaction and mutual dependency between the services and supporting services in the service catalogue, and monitoring the CMS.

*Inputs and outputs*
Inputs:
- business information and organization plans
- IT plans and financial plans
- Business Impact Analysis (BIA)
- service portfolio

Outputs:
- service definition
- updates for service portfolio
- service catalogue

## 4.2.2 Service Level Management

*Introduction*

The objective of the Service Level Management (SLM) process is to agree on the delivery of IT services and to make sure that the agreed level of IT service provision is attained.

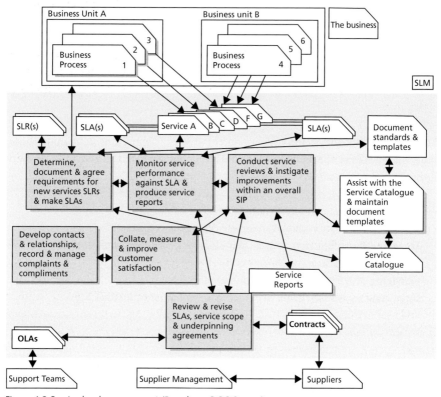

Figure 4.2 Service level management (Based on: OGC Source)

*Basic concepts*

The SLM process entails planning, coordinating, supplying, agreeing, monitoring and reporting on **Service Level Agreements (SLAs)**. This also includes the ongoing review of the service This ensures that the quality of the service satisfies the agreed requirements and can be improved where possible. The SLA is a written agreement between the

Service Provider and a customer containing mutual goals and responsibilities. Options for SLAs are:

- **Service-based SLAs** - Covers one service for all the customers of that service.
- **Customer-based SLAs** - An agreement with an individual customer group, covering all the services they use.
- **Multi-level SLAs** - For example a three-layer structure on corporate level, customer level and service level.

An **Operational Level Agreement (OLA)** is an agreement between an IT service provider and another part of the same organization. An OLA defines the goods or services to be provided from one department to the other, and the responsibilities of both parties.

An **Underpinning Contract (UC)** is a contract with a third party, in support of the delivery of an agreed IT service to a customer. The UC defines targets and responsibilities that are required to meet agreed service level targets in an SLA.

*Activities*
The activities of service level management (Figure 4.2) are:

- **Design of SLM Frameworks** - SLM has to design the best possible SLA, so that all services can be provided and clients can be serviced in a manner that meets mutual needs.
- **Determining, documenting and agreeing on the requirements for new services and production of Service Level Requirements (SLRs)** - When the service catalogue is made and the SLA structure determined, the first SLR (a customer requirement for an aspect of a service) needs to be determined.
- **Monitoring the performance with regard to the SLA and reporting the outcome** - Everything incorporated into the SLA must be measurable. Otherwise, disputes may arise, which may result in damaged confidence. Periodic reports must be produced with details of performance against SLA targets. A useful technique is to include a **SLA Monitoring (SLAM)** chart at the front of the report to give an 'at-a-glance' overview of how achievements have measured up against targets. These are most effective if colour coded Red, Amber, Green, and sometimes referred to as RAG charts as a result.
- **Improving client satisfaction** - Besides the "hard" criteria it should also be noted how the customer experiences the service rendered, in terms of "soft" criteria.
- **Review of the underlying agreements** - The IT service provider is also dependent on its own internal technical services and external partners; in order to satisfy the SLA targets, the underlying agreements with internal departments (OLAs) and external suppliers (UCs) must support the SLA.

- **Reviewing and improving services** - Regularly consult the customer to evaluate the services (**service reviews**) and make possible improvements in the service provision; focus on those improvement items that yield the greatest benefit to the business. Improvement activities should be documented and managed in a Service Improvement Plan (SIP).
- **Developing contacts and relationships** - SLM has to instill confidence in the business. With the service catalogue, SLM can start working proactively; the catalogue supplies information that improves the understanding of the relation between services, business units and processes.

*Inputs and outputs*
Inputs:
- information arising from strategic planning
- Business Impact Analysis (BIA)
- service portfolio and service catalogue

Outputs:
- service reports
- Service Improvement Plan (SIP)
- standard document templates
- SLA, SLR and OLAs
- Service quality plan

### 4.2.3   Capacity Management

*Introduction*
Capacity management has to provide IT capacity coinciding with both the current and future needs of the customers balanced against justifiable costs. Service Strategy analyzes the wishes and requirements of customers; in the Service Design phase, capacity management is a critical success factor for defining an IT service.

*Basic concepts*
The **Capacity Management Information System (CMIS)** provides relevant information on the capacity and performance of services in order to support the capacity management process. This information system is one of the most important elements in the capacity management process.

A **Capacity Plan** is used to manage the resources required to deliver IT services. It contains scenarios for different predictions of business demand, and costed options to deliver the agreed service level targets.

*Activities*
The capacity management process consists of:
- **reactive activities**:
  - monitoring and measuring
  - responding and reacting to capacity related events
- **proactive activities**:
  - predicting future requirements and trends
  - budgeting, planning and implementing upgrades
  - seeking ways to improve service performance
  - optimizing the performance of a service

Some activities must be executed repeatedly (proactively or reactively). They provide basic information and triggers for other activities and processes in capacity management. For instance:
- Monitoring IT usage and response times.
- Analyzing data.
- Tuning and implementation.

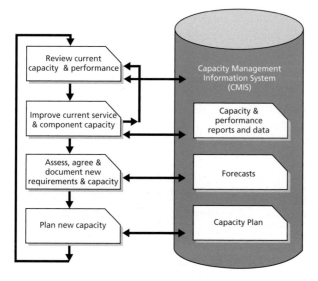

Figure 4.3 The capacity management process (Based on: OGC source)

Capacity management can be a extremely technical, complex and demanding process that comprises three sub-processes (Figure 4.4):

- **Business capacity management** - Translates the customer's requirements into specifications for the service and IT infrastructure; focus on current and future requirements.
- **Service capacity management** - Identifies and understands the IT services (including the sources, patterns, etc) to make them comply with the defined targets.
- **Component Capacity Management (CCM)** - Manages, controls and predicts the performance, use and capacity of individual IT components.

All of the capacity management sub-processes analyze the information stored in the CMIS.

*Inputs and outputs*
Inputs:
- Business information, including information from the organization plans (financial and IT-related)
- service and IT information
- change information from change management.

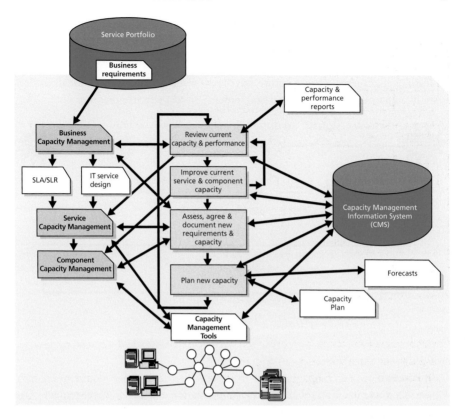

Figure 4.4 Sub-processes of capacity management (Based on: OGC source)

Outputs:
• Capacity Management Information System (CMIS)
• capacity plan (information on the current usage of the services and components)
• analyses of workload

#### 4.2.4 Availability Management

*Introduction*
Availability management has to ensure that the delivered availability levels for all services comply with or exceed the agreed requirements in a cost-effective manner.

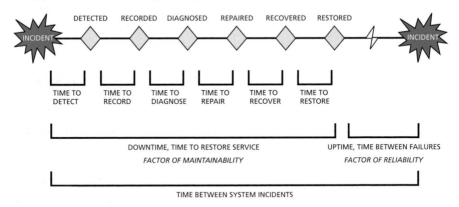

Figure 4.5 The extended incident lifecycle

*Basic concepts*
Figure 4.5 illustrates a number of starting points for availability management. The unavailability of services can be reduced by aiming to reduce each of the phases distinguished in the **extended incident lifecycle**.

Services must be restored quickly when they are unavailable to users. The **Mean Time to Restore Service (MTRS)** is the time within which a function (service, system or component) is back up after a failure. The MTRS depends on a number of factors, such as:

- configuration of service assets
- MTRS of individual components
- competencies of support personnel
- available resources
- policy plans
- procedures
- redundancy

Other metrics for measuring availability include:

- **Mean Time Between Failures (MTBF)** - The average time that a CI or service can perform its agreed function without interruption.
- **Mean Time Between Service Incidents (MTBSI)** - The mean time from when a system or service fails, until it next fails.
- **Mean Time To Repair (MTTR)** - The average time taken to repair a CI or service after a failure. MTTR is measured from when the CI or service fails until it is repaired. MTTR does not include the time required to recover or restore.

The **reliability** of a **service** or **component** indicates how long it can perform its agreed function without interruption.

The **maintainability** of a service or component indicates how fast it can be restored after a failure.

The **serviceability** describes the ability of a third party supplier to meet the terms of their contract, which includes agreed levels of reliability, maintainability or availability for a CI.

The reliability of systems can be increased through various types of **redundancy**.

Due to increased dependency upon IT services, customers often require services with **high availability**. This requires a design that considers the elimination of Single Points of Failure (SPOFs) and/or the provision of alternative components to provide minimal disruption to the business operation should an IT component failure occur.
High Availability solutions make use of techniques such as Fault Tolerance, resilience and fast recovery to reduce the number of incidents, and the impact of incidents.

**Service availability** involves all aspects of service availability and unavailability and the impact of component availability, or the potential impact of component unavailability on service availability. **Component availability** involves all aspects of component availability and unavailability.

*Activities*
Availability management must continually ensure that all services comply with the objectives. New or changed services must be designed in such a way that they comply with the objectives. To realize this, availability management can perform reactive and proactive activities (Figure 4.6):

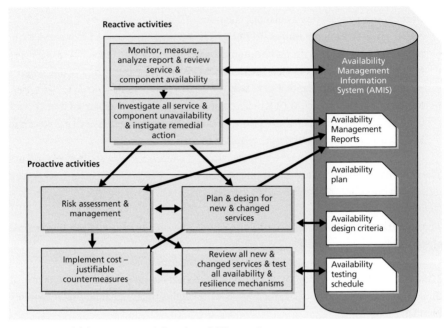

Figure 4.6 Availability management (Based on: OGC source)

- **Reactive activities** - Executed in the operational phase of the lifecycle:
  - monitoring, measuring, analyzing and reporting the availability of services and components
  - unavailability analysis
  - expanded lifecycle of the incident
  - Service Failure Analysis (SFA)
- **Proactive activities** - Executed in the design phase of the lifecycle:
  - identifying Vital Business Functions (VBFs)
  - designing for availability
  - Component Failure Impact Analysis (CFIA)
  - Single Point of Failure (SPOF) analysis
  - Fault Tree Analysis (FTA)
  - modeling to test and analyze predicted availabilities
  - risk analysis and management
  - availability test schemes
  - planned and preventive maintenance
  - production of the Projected Service Availability (PSA) document
  - continuous reviewing and improvement

## Inputs and outputs

Inputs:

- Business information, such as organization strategies, (financial) plans and information on the current and future requirements of IT services.
- Risk analyses, Business Impact Analyses (BIA) and studies of Vital Business Functions.
- Service information from the service portfolio and service catalogue and from the SLM process.
- Change calendars and release schemas from change management and release and deployment management.

Outputs:

- the Availability Management Information System (AMIS)
- the availability plan
- availability and restore design criteria
- reports on the availability, reliability and maintainability of services

### 4.2.5   IT Service Continuity Management

*Introduction*

IT Service Continuity Management (ITSCM) has to support business continuity by ensuring that the required IT facilities (computer systems, networks, etc.) can be resumed within the agreed timeframe.

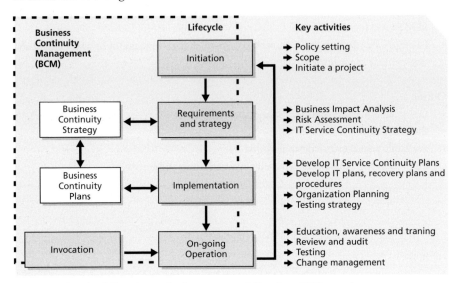

Figure 4.7 Lifecycle of IT service continuity management (Based on: OGC source)

*Basic concepts*

Once service continuity or recovery plans have been created they need to be (kept) aligned with the **Business Continuity Plans (BCPs)** and business priorities. Figure 4.7 shows the cyclic process of ITSCM and the role of overall **Business Continuity Management (BCM)**.

*Activities*

The process consists of four phases (Figure 4.7):

- **Initiation** - This phase covers the entire organization and includes the following activities:
  - defining the policy
  - specifying the conditions and scope
  - allocating resources (people, resources and funds)
  - defining the project organization and management structure
  - approving project and quality plans

- **Requirements and strategies** - Determining the business requirements for ITSCM is vital when investigating how well an organization can survive a calamity. This phase includes requirements and strategy. The requirements involve the performance of a Business Impact Analysis and risk estimate:
  - Requirement 1: Business Impact Analysis (BIA) - Quantify the impact caused by the loss of services. If the impact can be determined in detail, it is called "hard impact" - e.g. financial losses. "Soft impact" is less easily determined. It represents, for instance, the impact on Public Relations, morale and health.
  - Requirement 2: Risk estimate - There are various risk analyses and methods. Risk analysis is an assessment of risks that may occur. Risk management identifies the response and counter-measures that can be taken. A standard method like Management of Risk (M_o_R) can be used to investigate and manage the risks.
  - Strategy 1: Risk-reducing measures - Measures to reduce risks must be implemented in combination with availability management since failure reduction has an impact on service availability. Measures may include: fault tolerant systems, good IT security controls, and off-site storage.
  - Strategy 2: IT recovery options - The continuity strategy must weigh the costs of risk reducing measures against the recovery measures (manual work-arounds, reciprocal arrangements, gradual recovery, intermediate recovery, fast recovery and immediate recovery) to restore critical processes.
- **Implementation** - The ITSCM plans can be created once the strategy is approved. The organization structure (leadership and decision-making processes) changes in a disaster recovery process. Set this up around a senior manager in charge.
- **Operationalization** - This phase includes:
  - education, awareness and training of personnel
  - review and audit
  - testing
  - change management (ensures that all changes have been studied for their potential impact)
  - ultimate test (invocation)

*Inputs and outputs*

Inputs:

- business information (organization strategy, plans)
- IT information
- financial information
- change information (from change management)

Outputs:
- reviewed ITSCM policy
- Business Impact Analysis (BIA)
- risk analyses
- plans for disaster recovery, testing and crisis management

## 4.2.6 Information Security Management

*Introduction*
Information security management needs to align IT security with business security and has to ensure that information security is managed effectively in all services and service management operations.

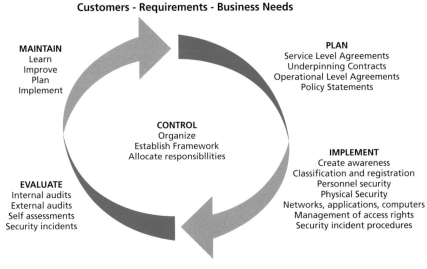

Figure 4.8 Framework for managing IT security (Based on: OGC source)

*Basic concepts*
The information security management process and framework include:
- information security policy
- **Information Security Management System (ISMS)**
- comprehensive security strategy (related to the business objectives and strategy)
- effective security structure and controls
- risk management
- monitoring processes
- communication strategy
- training strategy

The ISMS represents the basis for cost-effective development of an information security program that supports the business objectives. Use the **four Ps** of People, Processes, Products (including technology) and Partners (including suppliers) to ensure a high security level where required.

The framework can be based on ISO 27001, the international standard for information security management. Figure 4.8 is based on various recommendations, including ISO 27001, and provides information about the five elements (Control, Plan, Implement, Evaluate, Maintain) and their separate objectives.

*Activities*

Information security management should include the following activities:
- Operation, maintenance and distribution of an information security policy.
- Communication, implementation and enforcement of security policies
- Assessment of information.
- Implementing (and documenting) controls that support the information security policy and manage risks.
- Monitoring and management of breaches and incidents.
- Proactive improvement of the control systems.

The information security manager must understand that security is not just a step in the lifecycle and that it cannot be guaranteed by technology alone. Information security is a continuous process and an integrated part of all services and systems. Figure 4.9 describes controls that can be used in the process.

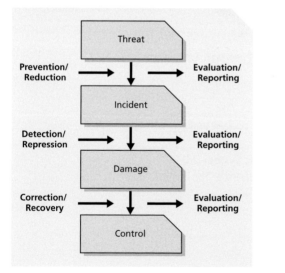

Figure 4.9 Security controls for threats and incidents (Based on: OGC source)

Figure 4.9 shows that a risk may result in a threat that in turn causes an incident, leading to damage. Various measures can be taken between these phases:
- **preventive measures** - prevent effects (e.g. access management)
- **reductive measures** - limit effects (e.g. backup and testing)
- **detective measures** - detect effects (e.g. monitoring)
- **repressive measures** - suppress effects (e.g. blocking)
- **corrective measures** - repair effects (e.g. rollback)

*Inputs and outputs*
Inputs:
- business information (strategy, plans)
- information from the SLM process
- change information from the change management process

Outputs:
- general information security management policy
- Information security management system
- security controls, audits and reports

### 4.2.7  Supplier Management

*Introduction*
Supplier management manages suppliers and the services they provide, it is aimed at securing consistent quality at the right price.

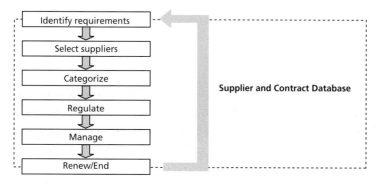

Figure 4.10 Contract lifecycle (Based on: OGC source)

*Basic concepts*
A **supplier** is a third party responsible for supplying goods or services that are required to deliver IT services.

A **contract** is a legally binding agreement between two or more parties.

All activities in this process must result from the supplier strategy and the Service Strategy policy. Create a **Supplier and Contract Database (SCD)** to achieve consistency and effectiveness in implementing policy. Ideally, this database would be an integrated element of CMS or SKMS. The database should contain all details regarding suppliers and their contracts, together with details about the type of service or product, and any information and relationships to other configuration items.

The data stored here will provide important information for activities and procedures such as:
- categorizing of suppliers
- maintenance of supplier and contract database
- evaluation and building of new suppliers and contracts
- building new supplier relationships
- management of suppliers and contracts
- renewing and ending contracts

*Activities*

In case of external suppliers, it is recommended that you draw up a formal contract with clearly defined, agreed upon and documented responsibilities and goals. You must manage this contract during its entire lifecycle (Figure 4.10).

These phases are:
1. **Identify business requirements**:
   - Produce a program of requirements.
   - Provide conformity of strategy and policy.
   - Develop a business case.
2. **Evaluate and select new suppliers** - Identify new business requirements and evaluate new suppliers as part of the Service Design process. They provide inputs for all other aspects of the lifecycle of the contract. Take various issues into account when selecting a new supplier, such as references, ability, and financial aspects.
3. **Categorizing suppliers and contracts** - The amount of time and energy that should be put into a supplier depends on the impact of this supplier and its service. A subdivision could be made according to strategic relationships (managed by senior management), relationships at a tactical level (managed by middle management), execution level (execution management) and suppliers that only provide goods such as paper and cartridges.
4. **Introduce new suppliers and contracts** - In order to present a clear image of the impact of new suppliers and contracts, the change management process must add them to the Supplier and Contract Database. A Business Impact Analysis (BIA) and risk assessment, in combination with ITSCM, availability management and information security management, could be good methods to clarify the impact of new contracts on various business units.
5. **Manage performance of suppliers and contracts** - At an operational level, the integrated processes of the client organization and of the supplier must function efficiently. Questions should be:
   - Should the supplier conform to the organization's change management process?
   - How will the service desk inform the supplier if there are incidents?
   - How will CMS information be updated when CIs change?

   During the lifecycle of the contract, keep a close eye on the following two issues in order to minimize risks:
   - the performance of suppliers
   - the services, service scope and contract reviews in comparison with original business requirements

   Make sure that provisions are still in tune with what the business initially desired.

6. **Renew or end contract** - At a strategic level, see how the contract is functioning and how relevant it will be in the future, whether changes are necessary and what the commercial performance of the contract is. Benchmarking could be an appropriate instrument to compare the current service provision with that of other suppliers in the industry. If, as a result, the decision is made to end the relationship with the supplier, it is important to assess what the consequences will be in legal and financial areas, and how the client organization and service provision will be affected.

*Inputs and outputs*
Inputs:
- business information (strategy, plans)
- supplier and contract strategies
- business plan details

Outputs:
- Supplier and Contract Database (SCD)
- information about performance
- supplier improvement plans (Supplier Service Improvement Plans, SIPs)
- research reports

## 4.3  Sample Questions

1. Which of the following statements is NOT an objective of Service Design?
   a. To design services to satisfy business objectives.
   b. To identify and manage risks.
   c. To plan and manage the resources to successfully establish a new or changed service into production with the predicted cost, quality and time estimates.
   d. To design efficient and effective processes for the design, transition, operation and improvement of high-quality IT services.

2. Which of the following statements are CORRECT?
   a. A Service Provider is an organization supplying services to one or more external customers.
   b. A Service Provider is an organization supplying services to one or more internal customers or external customers.
   c. A Service Provider is a third party responsible for supplying goods or underpinning services that are required to deliver IT services.
   d. A Service Provider is a role that has responsibility for ensuring that all new services are designed to deliver the levels of availability required by the business and validation of the final design to meet the minimum levels of availability as agreed by the business for IT services.

3. Which of the following are the five major aspects of Service Design?
   1. Service Portfolio design
   2. Technology and architectural design
   3. Design of services
   4. Strategy design
   5. Process design
   6. Measurement design
   a. 1, 2, 3, 4 and 5
   b. 1, 2, 4, 5 and 6
   c. 1, 2, 3, 5 and 6
   d. 2, 3, 4, 5 and 6

4. Which of the following is NOT a sourcing approach?
   a. Insourcing
   b. Co-sourcing
   c. Rightsourcing
   d. Application Service Provision

5. Which of the following activities is an activity in the Service Level Management process?
   a. Collate, measure and improve customer satisfaction
   b. Status reporting
   c. Deploy Service Component
   d. Resolution and Recovery

6. Which of the following metrics is BEST used to judge the efficiency and effectiveness of the Service Level Management process?
   a. Number and percentage of major incidents.
   b. The number and severity of service breaches.
   c. Reduction in the number of disruptions to services caused by inaccurate impact assessment.
   d. Reduction in the costs of handling printer incidents.

7. Consider the following roles and responsibilities:
   A. Availability Manager
   B. Service Catalogue Manager
   C. Supplier Manager
   D. Capacity Manager
   1. Analysis of usage and performance data, and reporting on performance against targets contained in Service Level Agreements.
   2. Ensuring that all of the information within the Service Catalog is consistent with the information within the Service Portfolio.
   3. Performing contract or Service Level Agreement reviews at least annually and ensuring that all contracts are consistent with organizational requirements and standard terms and conditions wherever possible.
   4. Ensuring that all existing services deliver the levels of availability agreed with the business in Service Level Agreements.
   Which of the following pairings between the roles and responsibilities is CORRECT?
   a. A-1, B-3, C-2 and D-4
   b. A-1, B-2, C-3 and D-4
   c. A-2, B-3, C-4 and D-1
   d. A-4, B-2, C-3 and D-1

8. Which of the following is NOT a sub-process of the Capacity Management process?
   a. Component Capacity Management
   b. Configuration Capacity Management
   c. Business Capacity Management
   d. Service Capacity Management

9. In the RACI authority matrix the letter 'C' stands for:
    a. Classified
    b. Configured
    c. Consulted
    d. Communication

# CHAPTER 5

# Service Transition

## 5.1 Lifecycle Phase

### 5.1.1 Introduction

Service Transition consists of the management and coordination of the processes, systems and functions required for the building, testing and deployment of new and changed services. Service Transition establishes the services as specified in the Service Design phase, based on the customer and stakeholder requirements.

A Service Transition is effective and efficient if the transition delivers what the business requested within the limitations in terms of money and other necessary resources, as determined in the Service Design phase.

*Goals*
The **goals** of Service Transition include:
- supporting the change process of the business (client)
- reducing variations in the performance and known errors of the new/changed service
- ensuring the service meets the requirements of the service specifications

*Objectives*
The **objectives** of Service Transition include:
- the necessary means to realize, plan and manage the new service
- ensuring the minimum impact for the services which are already in production
- improving customer satisfaction and stimulate the proper use of the service and mutual technology

*Scope*
ITIL defines the **scope** of Service Transition as follows: Service Transition includes the management and coordination of the processes, systems and functions required for the packaging, building, testing and deployment of a release into production, and establish the service specified in the customer and stakeholder requirements.

Although change management, service asset and configuration management and knowledge management support all phases of the service lifecycle, the ITIL Service

Transition book covers these. Release and deployment management, service validation and testing, and evaluation are included in the scope of Service Transition.

*Value to the business*
An effective Service Transition ensures that the new or changed services are better aligned with the customer's business operation. Specifically:
- the capacity of the business to respond quickly and adequately to changes in the market
- changes in the business as a result of takeovers, contracting, etc. are well managed
- more successful changes and releases for the business
- better compliance of business and governing rules
- less deviation between planned budgets and the actual costs
- better insight into the possible risks during and after the input of a service
- higher productivity of customer staff

### 5.1.2   Basic concepts
The following **policies** are important for an effective Service Transition and apply to every organization. The approach does need to be adjusted to the conditions that are appropriate for each different organization:
- Define and implement guidelines and procedures for Service Transition.
- Implement all changes through Service Transition.
- Use common frameworks and standards.
- Re-use existing processes and systems.
- Coordinate Service Transition plans with the needs of the business.
- Create relations with stakeholders and maintain these.
- Set up effective controls on assets, responsibilities and activities.
- Deliver systems for knowledge transfer and decision support.
- Plan packages for releases and deployment.
- Anticipate and manage changes in plans.
- Manage the resources proactively.
- Continue to ensure the involvement of stakeholders at an early stage in the service lifecycle.
- Assure the quality of a new or changed services.
- Proactively improve service quality during a Service Transition.

### 5.1.3   Processes and other activities
A Service Transition generally comprises the following steps:
- planning and preparation
- building

- service testing and pilots
- planning and preparation of the deployment
- deployment, transition and retire
- review and closing of Service Transition

This section briefly explains the processes and activities of a Service Transition. More information about each of these processes can be found in Section 5.2 of this study guide.

Service Transition processes:
- **Transition planning and support** - Ensures the planning and coordination of resources in order to realize the specification of the Service Design.
- **Change management** - Ensures that changes are implemented in a controlled manner, i.e. that they are evaluated, prioritized, planned, tested, implemented, and documented.
- **Service Asset and Configuration Management (SACM)** - Manages the service assets and Configuration Items (CIs) in order to support the other service management processes.
- **Release and deployment management** - Aimed at the building, testing and deploying of the services specified in the Service Design, and ensures that the client can utilize the service effectively.
- **Service validation and testing** - Tests ensure that the new or changed services are "fit for purpose" and "fit for use".
- **Evaluation** - Generic process that is intended to verify whether the performance is acceptable; for example, whether it has the right price / quality ratio, whether it is continued, whether it is in use, whether it is paid for, and so on.
- **Knowledge management** - Improves the quality of decision-making (for management) by ensuring that reliable and safe information is available during the service lifecycle.

Service Transition activities:
- **Communication** is central during every Service Transition.
- Significant change of a service also means a change of the organization. **Organizational change management** should address **the emotional change cycle** (shock, avoidance, external blame, self-blame and acceptance), **culture and attitudes**.
- **Stakeholder management** is a Crucial Success Factor in Service Transition. A stakeholder analysis can be made to find out what the requirements and interests of the stakeholders are, and what their final influence and power will be during the transition.

Change management, SACM and knowledge management are whole service lifecycle processes but influence and support all lifecycle stages. Release and deployment management, service validation and testing, and evaluation are strongly focused within the Service Transition phase.

### 5.1.4  Organization

Service Transition is actively managed by a **service transition manager**. The service transition manager is responsible for the daily management and control of the Service Transition teams and their activities.

Generic **roles** are:
- **Process owner** - The process owner ensures that all process activities are carried out.
- **Service owner** - The service owner has the responsibility, toward the client, for the initiation, transition and maintenance of a service.

The most important **service transition roles** and **responsibilities** are discussed in the following section.

The responsibilities of the **service asset manager** include:
- formulating process objectives and implementing the policy, the process standards, plans and procedures
- evaluating the existing asset management systems and implementing the new systems
- indicating the scope and function of the process, which items must be managed and the information that must be established
- taking care of communication about the process and making it known
- taking care of resources and training
- setting up the identification and the naming conventions of assets
- taking care of the evaluation of the use of tooling
- setting up interfaces with other processes
- planning the completion of the asset database
- making reports
- assisting with audits and taking care of corrective actions

The responsibilities of the **configuration manager** include:
- formulating process objectives and implementing the policy, the process standards, plans and procedures

- evaluating the existing configuration management systems and implementing the new systems
- indicating the scope and function of the process, which items must be managed and the information that must be established
- taking care of communication about the process and making it known
- taking care of resources and training
- setting up the identification and the naming conventions of CIs
- taking care of the evaluation of the use of tooling
- setting up interfaces with other processes
- evaluating existing CMS systems and implementation of new systems
- planning the filling in of CMS in the CMDBs
- making reports
- assisting with audits and taking corrective actions

The responsibilities of the **configuration analyst** include:
- proposes scope of asset and configuration management
- train staff
- propose naming conventions
- create asset and configuration management processes and procedures
- perform configuration audits and checks

The responsibilities of the **configuration administrator/librarian** include:
- administer and guard all master copies of software, assets and documented CIs

The responsibilities of the **CMS/tools administrator** include:
- evaluation of proprietary asset and configuration management tools
- monitoring of performance and capacity of asset and configuration management systems
- ensuring the integrity and performance of asset and configuration management systems

The **change manager** has responsibilities (some of which can be delegated) including:
- receiving, logging and prioritizing (in collaboration with the initiator) RFCs, rejecting RFS based on the criteria
- preparing and chairing CAB and ECAB meetings
- deciding who attends which meeting, who receives RFCs, what must be changed there
- publishing Changes Schedules (SCs)
- maintaining change logs

---

- closing RFCs
- reviewing implemented changes
- making reports

The **Change Advisory Board (CAB)** is an advisory consultation body. The specific roles and responsibilities of the CAB will be explained in Section 5.2.

The responsibilities of the **release packaging and build manager** include:
- final release configuration
- building the final release and testing it (prior to independent testing)
- reporting known faults and workarounds
- input to the final implementation sign-off

The **deployment manager** is responsible for the following including:
- the final service implementation
- coordination of all release documentation, release notes and communication
- planning of the deployment, in combination with change management, knowledge management and SACM
- providing guidance during the release process
- giving feedback concerning the effectiveness of a release
- recording metrics for deployment to ensure within agreed SLAs

ITIL also recognizes the following roles in the Service Transition phase of the service lifecycle, but this falls outside the scope of this book and the ITIL Foundations Exams:
- configuration management team
- change authority
- risk-evaluation manager
- service knowledge manager
- test support
- Early Life Support (ELS)
- build and test environment management

### 5.1.5 Methods, techniques and tools
Technology plays an important part in the support of Service Transition. It can be divided into two types:
- **IT service management systems** - Such as enterprise frameworks which offer integration opportunities linking with the CMS or other tools; system, network and application management tools; service dashboard and reporting tools.

- **Specific ITSM technology and tools** - Such as service knowledge management systems; collaboration tools; tools for measuring and reporting; test (management) tools; publishing tools; release and deployment technology.

### 5.1.6 Implementation and operation

The implementation of Service Transition in a "Greenfield" situation (from zero) is only likely when establishing a new service provider. Most service providers therefore focus on the improvement of the existing Service Transition (processes and services). For the improvement of Service Transition the following five aspects are important:

1. **Justification** - Show the benefits in business terms of effective service transition to all stakeholders.
2. **Design** - Factors to take into account when designing are standards and guidelines, relationships with other supporting services, project and program management, resources, all stakeholders, budget and means.
3. **Introduction** - Do not apply the improved or newly implemented Service Transition to current projects.
4. **Cultural aspects** - Even formalizing existing procedures will lead to cultural changes in an organization. Take this into consideration.
5. **Risks and advantages** - Do not make any decisions about the introduction or improvement of Service Transition without an insight into the expected risks and advantages.

There is input/output of knowledge and experience from and to Service Transition. For example: Service Operation shares practical experiences with Service Transition as to how similar services behave in production. Also, experiences from Service Transition supply inputs for the assessment of the designs from Service Design. Like processes in a process model, all phases in a lifecycle will have outputs that are inputs in another phase of that lifecycle.

For a successful Service Transition, several challenges need to be conquered, such as:
- Taking into account the needs of all stakeholders.
- Finding a balance between a stable operating environment and being able to respond to changing business requirements.
- Creating a culture which is responsive to cooperation and cultural changes.
- Ensuring that the quality of services corresponds to the quality of the business.
- A clear definition of the roles and responsibilities.

Potential risks of Service Transition are:
- de-motivation of staff
- unforeseen expenses
- excessive cost
- resistance to changes
- lack of knowledge sharing
- poor integration between processes
- lack of maturity and integration of systems and tools

## 5.2 Functions and Processes

### 5.2.1 Transition Planning and Support

*Introduction*
Transition planning and support ensures the planning and coordination of resources in order to realize the specification of the Service Design. Transition planning and support plans changes and ensures that issues and risks are managed.

*Basic concepts*
The **Service Design Package (SDP)** that was created in the Service Design phase contains all aspects of an IT service and its requirements through each stage of its lifecycle. It includes the information about the execution of activities of the Service Transition team.

A **release policy** should be defined, in which the following subjects are addressed:
- naming conventions, distinguishing release types
- roles and responsibilities
- release frequency
- acceptance criteria for the various transition phases
- the criteria for leaving Early Life Support (ELS)

The following types of release can be defined:
- **Major release** - Important deployment of new hardware and software with, in most cases, a considerable expansion of the functionality.
- **Minor release** - These usually contain a number of smaller improvements; some of these improvements were previously implemented as quick fixes but are now included integrally within a release.
- **Emergency release** - Usually implemented as a temporary solution for a problem or known error.

*Activities*
The activities for planning are:
1. **Set up transition strategy** - The transition strategy defines the global approach to Service Transition and the assignment of resources.
2. **Prepare Service Transition** - The preparation consists of analysis and acceptance of input from other service lifecycle phases and other inputs; identifying, filing and planning RFCs; monitoring the baseline and transition readiness.

3. **Plan and coordinate Service Transition** - An individual Service Transition plan describes the tasks and activities required to roll out a release in a test and production environment.
4. **Support** - Service Transition advises and supports all stakeholders. The planning and support team will provide insight for the stakeholders regarding Service Transition processes and supporting systems and tools.

Finally, Service Transition activities are monitored: the implementation of activities is compared with the way they were intended.

*Inputs and outputs*
Inputs:
- authorized RFCs
- Service Design Package (SDP)
- definition of the release package and design specifications
- acceptance criteria for the service

Outputs:
- transition strategy
- integral collection of Service Transition plans

## 5.2.2   Change Management

*Introduction*

The primary objective of change management is to enable beneficial changes to be made, with minimal disruption to IT services. Change management ensures that changes are deployed in a controlled way, i.e. they are evaluated, prioritized, planned, tested, implemented and documented.

Changes are made for proactive or reactive reasons. Examples of proactive reasons are cost reduction and service improvement. Examples of reactive reasons for change are solving service disruptions and adapting the service to a changing environment.

The change management process must:
• use standardized methods and procedures
• record all changes in the CMS
• take account of risks for the business

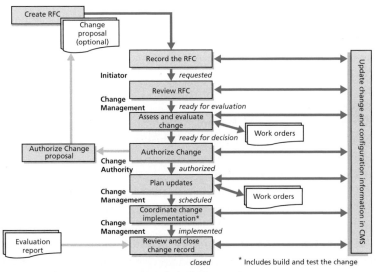

Figure 5.1 Change management (Based on: OGC source)

*Basic concepts*

A **Request for Change** (RFC) is a formal request to change one or more CIs.

Different types of change may require different **types of change request**. For example: an RFC to service portfolios, an RFC to service or service definition, a project change proposal, a user access request, an operational activity.

A **service change** is the addition, modification or elimination of an authorized, planned or supporting service (component) and its related documentation.

A **normal change** is a change that must follow the complete change process flow (see the next section 'Activities').

A **standard change** is a pre-approved, low risk and relatively common change. Standard changes must be registered by change management.

An **emergency change** is a change that must be introduced as soon as possible. For example, to repair a failure as soon as possible in an IT service that has a large negative impact on the business.

The **priority of the change** is based on impact and urgency. Change management schedules the changes on the change calendar: the Change Schedule (CS).

The **seven R's** of change management represent a good starting point for **impact analysis**:
1.  Who raised the change? (**Raised**)
2.  What is the reason for the change? (**Reason**)
3.  What is the return required from the change? (**Return**)
4.  What are the change's risks? (**Risk**)
5.  What resources does it require? (**Resources**)
6.  Who are responsible for build, testing and implementation? (**Responsible**)
7.  Which relationships exist between this and other changes? (**Relationship**)

The **Change Advisory Board (CAB)** is a consultative body that regularly meets to help the change manager assess, prioritize and schedule the changes. In case of emergency changes, it can be necessary to identify a smaller organization to make emergency decisions: the **Emergency CAB (ECAB)**.

No change should be approved without having a **remediation plan** for **back out**.

A **Post-Implementation Review (PIR)** should be carried out to determine whether the change was successful and to identify opportunities for improvement.

*Activities*

The specific activities (see Figure 5.1) to manage individual changes in a **normal change** procedure are:

1. **Create and record** - An individual or department may submit an RFC. All RFCs are registered and must be identifiable.
2. **Review the RFC** - After registration, the stakeholders verify whether the RFC is illogical, unfeasible, unnecessary or incomplete, or whether it has already been submitted earlier.
3. **Assess and evaluate changes** - Based on the impact, risk assessment, potential benefits and costs of the change, the change authority determines whether a change is implemented or not.
4. **Authorize the change** - For every change there is a formal authorization required. This may be a role, person or group of people.
5. **Coordinate implementation** - Forward approved changes to the relevant product experts, so that they can build and test the changes, and create and deploy releases.
6. **Evaluate and close** - Implemented changes are evaluated after some time (**Post-Implementation Review (PIR)**). If the change is successful, it can be closed.

*Inputs and outputs*

Inputs:
- RFCs
- change, transition, release and deployment plans
- Change Schedule and Projected Service Outage (PSO, document that explains effects of planned changes/maintenance on service levels)
- assets and CIs
- evaluation report

Outputs:
- rejected or approved RFCs
- new or changed services, CIs, assets
- adjusted PSO
- updated Change Schedule
- change decisions, actions, documents, records and reports

### 5.2.3  Service Asset and Configuration Management

*Introduction*

Service Asset and Configuration Management (SACM) manages the service assets and Configuration Items (CIs) in order to support the other service management processes. SACM defines the service and infrastructure components and maintains accurate configuration records.

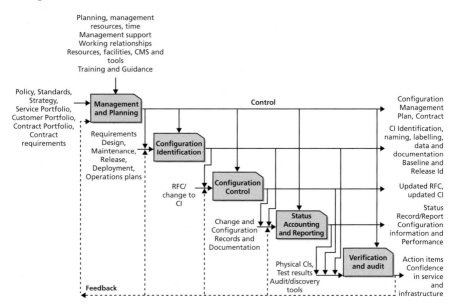

Figure 5.2 Service asset and configuration management (Based on: OGC source)

*Basic concepts*

A **Configuration Item (CI)** is an asset, service component or other item that is (or will be) controlled by configuration management.

An **attribute** is a piece of information about a CI. For example version number, name, location et cetera.

A **relationship** is a link between two CIs that identifies a dependency or connection between them. Relationships show how CIs work together to provide a service.

By maintaining relations between CIs a **logical configuration model** of the services, assets and infrastructure is created. This provides valuable information for other processes.

A **configuration structure** shows the relations and hierarchy between CIs that comprise a configuration.

Configuration management ensures that all CIs are provided with a **baseline** and that they are maintained. A **configuration management baseline** can be used to restore the IT infrastructure to a known configuration if a change or release fails.

CIs are **classified** (the act of assigning a category to a CI) to help manage and trace them throughout their lifecycles, for instance: service, hardware, software, documentation, staff.

A **Configuration Management Database** (CMDB) is a database used to store configuration records of CIs. One or more CMDBs can be part of a Configuration Management System.

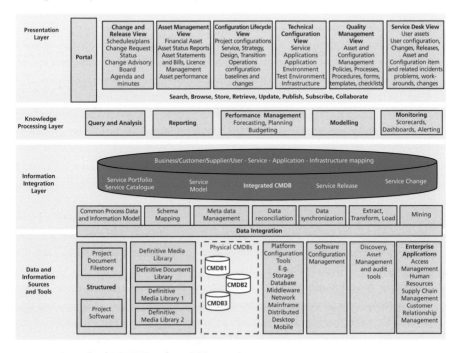

Figure 5.3 Example of a CMS (Based on: OGC source)

In order to manage large and complex IT services and infrastructures SACM needs to use a supporting system: the **Configuration Management System (CMS)**.

Various **libraries** are defined:
- A **secure library** is a collection of software and electronic CIs (documents) of a known type and status.
- A **secure store** is a secure location where IT assets are stored.

The **Definitive Media Library (DML)** is a secure store where the definitive, authorized (approved) versions of all media CIs are stored and monitored.

**Definitive spares** are spare components and assemblies that are maintained at the same level as the comparative systems within the live environment.

A **snapshot** ("moment in time") is the state of a configuration at a certain point in time (for instance when it was inventoried by a discovery tool). It can be recorded in the CMS to remain as a fixed historical record of the configuration, not necessarily authorized.

*Activities*

The basic SACM process activities consist of:
1. **Management and planning** - The management team and configuration management decide what level of configuration management is needed and how this level will be achieved. This is documented in a configuration management plan.
2. **Configuration identification** - Configuration identification focuses on establishing a CI classification system. Configuration identification determines: the configuration structures and selection of CIs; the naming conventions of CIs, the CI labels; relations between CIs, the relevant attributes of CIs, type of CIs et cetera.
3. **Configuration control** - Configuration control ensures that the CIs are adequately controlled. No CIs can be added, adapted, replaced or removed without following the agreed procedure.
4. **Status accounting and reporting** - The lifecycle of a component is classified into different stages. For example: development or draft, approved and withdrawn. The stages that different types of CIs go through must be properly documented and the status of each CI must be tracked.
5. **Verification and audit** - SACM conducts audits to ensure that there are no discrepancies between the documented baselines and the actual situation; and that release and configuration documentation is present before the release is rolled out.

*Inputs and outputs*

Updates to assets and CIs are triggered by RFCs, service requests and incidents.

## 5.2.4   Release and Deployment Management

*Introduction*
Release and deployment management is aimed at building, testing and delivering the capability to provide the services specified by Service Design.

*Basic concepts*
A **release** is a set of new or changed CIs that are tested and will be implemented into production together.

A **release unit** is a part of the service or infrastructure that is included in the release, in accordance with the organization's release guidelines.

In the **release design** different considerations apply in respect of the way in which the release is deployed. The most frequently occurring options for the rollout of releases are: "**big bang**" versus **phased**, "**push and pull**", **automated** or **manual**.

A **release package** is a single release unit or (structured) collection of release units. All the elements of which the service consists - the infrastructure, hardware, software, applications, documentation, knowledge, et cetera - must be taken into account.

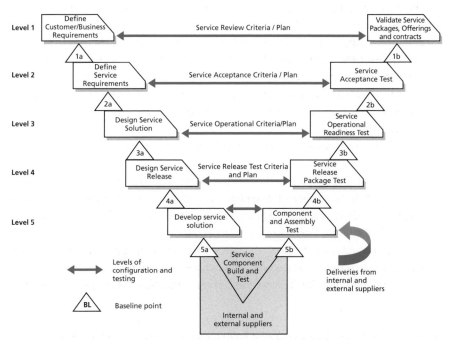

Figure 5.4 The service V model (Based on: OGC source)

The **V model** (Figure 5.4) is a convenient tool for mapping out the different configuration levels at which building and testing must take place. The left side of the V in this example starts with service specifications and ends with the detailed Service Design. The right side of the V reflects the test activities, by means of which the specifications on the left-hand side must be validated. In the middle we find the test and validation criteria (See the section "Service validation and testing").

*Activities*
The process activities of release and deployment management are:

1.  **Planning** - Prior to a deployment into production different plans are formulated. The type and number depends on the size and complexity of the environment and the changed or new service.
2.  **Preparation for building (compilation), testing and deployment** - Before approval can be given for the building and test phase, the service and release design is compared against the specifications of the new or changed service (validation).
3.  **Building and testing** - The building and test phase of the release consists of the management of general (common) infrastructure and services; use of release and building documentation; acquisition, purchasing and testing of CIs and components for the release; compilation of the release (release packaging); structuring and controlling the test environments.
4.  **Service testing and pilots** - Test management is responsible for the coordination of the test activities and the planning and control of the implementation.
5.  **Planning and preparing the deployment** - This activity evaluates the extent to which each deployment team is prepared (readiness assessment) for the deployment.
6.  **Transfer, deployment, and retirement** - The following activities are important during deployment: the transfer of financial assets; transfer and transition of business and organization; transfer of service management resources; transfer of the service; deployment of the service; retirement of services; removal of superfluous assets.
7.  **Verify deployment** - When all the deployment activities have been completed it is important to verify that all stakeholders are able to use the service as intended.
8.  **Early life support** - Early Life Support (ELS) is intended to offer extra support after the deployment of a new or changed service.
9.  **Review and close** - In the review of a deployment, check whether the knowledge transfer and training were adequate; all user experiences have been documented; all fixes and changes are complete and all problems, known errors and workarounds have been documented; the quality criteria have been complied with; the service is ready for transition from ELS into production.

*Inputs and outputs*

Inputs:

- approved RFC, service package, SLP, SDP, continuity plans
- release policies, design and model, construction model and plan
- technology, purchasing, service management and operation standards and plans
- exit and entry criteria for each phase of the release and deployment

Outputs:

- release and deployment plans, completed RFC, service notifications, an updated service catalogue and service model
- new or changed service management documentation and service reports
- new tested service environment
- SLA, OLAs and contracts
- Service Transition report and service capacity plan
- Complete CI list of release package

### 5.2.5   Service Validation and Testing

*Introduction*
Testing of services during the service transition phase ensures that the new or changed services are **fit for purpose (utility)** and **fit for use (warranty)**.

The goal of service validation and testing is to ensure the delivery of *that* added value that is agreed and expected. When not properly tested, additional incidents, problems and costs will occur.

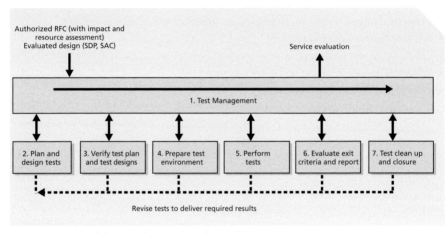

Figure 5.5 Service validation and testing (Based on: OGC source)

*Basic concepts*
The **service model** describes the structure and dynamics of a service provided by Service Operation. The structure consists of main and supporting services and service assets. When a new or changed service is designed, developed and built, these service assets are tested in relation to design specifications and requirements. Activities, flow of resources, coordination, and interactions describe the dynamics.

The **test strategy** defines the entire testing approach and the allocation of required resources.

A **test model** consists of a test plan, the object to be tested and test scripts which indicate the method by which each element must be tested.

The **Service Design Package (SDP)** defines **entry and exit criteria** for all test perspectives.

By using **test models**, such as a **V model** (see Figure 5.4), testing becomes a part of the service lifecycle early in the process.

**Fit for purpose** means that the service does what the client expects of it, so that the service supports the business. **Fit for use** addresses such aspects as availability, continuity, capacity and security of the service.

In addition to all kinds of functional and non-functional **test types**, **role playing** is also possible based on perspective (target group).

*Activities*
The following test activities can be distinguished:
- **Validation and test management** - Test management consists of planning and managing (control), and reporting on the activities taking place during all test phases of the Service Transition.
- **Planning and design** - Test planning and design activities take place early in the service lifecycle and relate to resources, supporting services, planning milestones and delivery and acceptance.
- **Verification of test plan and design** - Test plans and designs are verified to make sure that everything (including scripts) is complete, and that test models sufficiently take into account the risk profile of the service in question, and all possible interfaces.
- **Preparation of the test environment** - Prepare the test environment and make a baseline of the test environment.
- **Testing** - The tests are executed using manual or automated testing techniques and procedures. Testers register all results.
- **Evaluate exit criteria and report** - The actual results are compared with projected results (exit criteria).
- **Clean up and closure** - Make sure that the test environment is cleaned. Evaluate the test approach and determine issues that need improvement.

*Inputs and outputs*
Inputs:
- the service and Service Level Package (SLP)
- interface definitions by the supplier
- Service Design Package (SDP)
- release and deployment plans
- acceptance criteria and RFCs

Outputs:
- test report, test incidents, test problems, test errors
- improvement (for CSI)
- updated data
- information and knowledge for the knowledge management system

### 5.2.6   Evaluation

*Introduction*

Evaluation is a generic process that is intended to verify whether the performance of "something" is acceptable; for example, whether it has the right price/quality ratio, whether it is continued, whether it is in use, whether it is paid for, and so on.

Evaluation delivers important input for Continual Service Improvement (CSI) and future improvement of service development and change management.

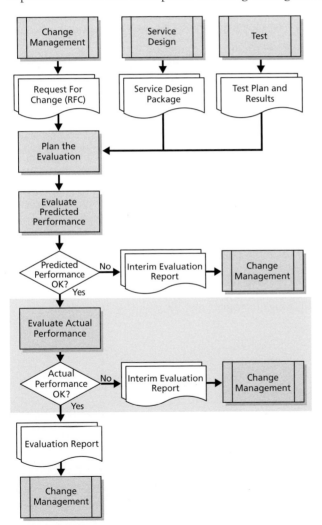

Figure 5.6 Evaluation (Based on: OGC source)

*Basic concepts*
An **evaluation report** contains a risk profile, a deviations report, a qualification and validation statement (if necessary), and a recommendation (to accept or refuse the change).

The **predicted performance** of a service is the expected performance. The **actual performance** is the performance following a service change.

*Activities*
The evaluation process consists of the following activities:

1. **Planning the evaluation** - When planning an evaluation, the intended and unintended effects of a change are analyzed.
2. **Evaluating the predicted performance** - Perform a risk assessment based on the customer's specifications, the predicted performance and the performance model. Send an interim assessment report to change management if the evaluation shows that the predicted performance represents an unacceptable risk to the change or deviates from the acceptance criteria. Cease the evaluation activities while awaiting a decision from change management.
3. **Evaluating the actual performance** - After implementation of the service change, Service Operation reports on the actual performance of the service. Perform a second risk assessment, again based on the customer's specifications, the predicted performance and the performance model. Send a new interim assessment report to change management if the evaluation shows that the actual performance represents an unacceptable risk and cease the evaluation activities while awaiting a decision from change management.

Send an evaluation report to change management if the evaluation is approved.

*Inputs and outputs*
Inputs:
- RFCs
- the Service Design Package (SDP)
- Service Acceptance Criteria (SACs)
- test plans and results

Output:
- The evaluation report

## 5.2.7  Knowledge Management

### Introduction

Knowledge management improves the quality of decision-making by ensuring that reliable and safe information is available during the service lifecycle.

Effective sharing of knowledge requires the development and maintenance of a Service Knowledge Management System (SKMS). This system should be available to all information stakeholders and suit all information requirements.

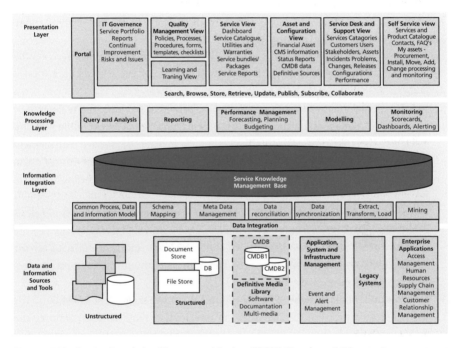

Figure 5.7 The Service Knowledge Management System (SKMS) (Based on: OGC source)

### Basic concepts

Knowledge management is often visualized using the **DIKW** structure: Data-Information-Knowledge-Wisdom. Quantitative data from metrics are transformed into qualitative information. By combining information with experience, context, interpretation and reflection it becomes knowledge. Ultimately, knowledge can be used to make the right decisions which comes down to wisdom.

The basis of the **Service Knowledge Management System (SKMS)** is formed by a considerable amount of data in a central database or Configuration Management System (CMS) and the CMDB: the CMDB feeds the CMS and the CMS provides input for the SKMS and so supports the decision-making process. However, the scope of the SKMS is broader. Information is also stored that relates to matters such as:

- the experience and skills of staff
- information about peripheral issues such as the behavior of users and the performance of the organization
- requirements and expectations of suppliers and partners

There are a number of knowledge transfer techniques, such as learning styles; knowledge visualization; driving behavior; seminars; advertisements; newsletter, newspaper.

*Activities*

Knowledge management consists of the following activities, methods and techniques:

1. **Knowledge management strategy** - An organization needs an overall knowledge management strategy. If such a strategy is already in place, the service management knowledge strategy can link into it. The knowledge management strategy also focuses specifically on on identifying and documenting relevant knowledge, and on the data and information that support this knowledge.

2. **Knowledge transfer** - The transfer of knowledge is a challenging task that requires, in the first place, an analysis to determine what the knowledge gap is between the department or person in possession of the knowledge and those in need of the knowledge. Based on the outcome of this analysis, a communication (improvement) plan is formulated to facilitate the knowledge transfer.

3. **Information management** - Data and information management consists of the following activities: establishing data and information requirements; defining the information architecture; establishing data and information management procedures; evaluation and improvement.

4. **Use of the SKMS** - Supplying services to customers in different time zones and regions and with different operating hours imposes strenuous requirements on the sharing of knowledge. For this reason the supplier must develop and maintain an SKMS system that is available to all stakeholders and suits all information requirements.

*Inputs and outputs*

Each organization has it own specific knowledge requirements. However, these organizations share the requirement to manage the transfer of that knowledge and information between phases and amongst staff.

Service delivery errors discovered during transition are recorded and analyzed. Service Transition makes the information about the consequences of these errors and any workarounds available to Service Operation.

Service Transition staff also collect information and data that is returned to Service Design via CSI, and feedback information to Service Design if a change in approach is needed.

Operations staff, such as incident management staff and first and second line staff, are the central "collection point" for information about the day-to-day routine of the managed services. It is essential that this information and knowledge is documented and transferred. Staff who are working in problem management are important users of this knowledge.

## 5.3 Sample Questions

1. Service Transition adds value to the business by improving:
   a. the management of the technology that is used to deliver and support services
   b. the success rate of changes and releases for the business
   c. the design of the IT processes
   d. the organizational competency for Continual Service Improvement

2. Which of the following is NOT a Change type?
   a. Normal Change
   b. Emergency Change
   c. Known Change
   d. Standard Change

3.  Which of the following statements about the Service V model are CORRECT?
    1.  Using a model such as the V model builds in service validation and testing early in the Service Lifecycle.
    2.  The left-hand side of the V model represents the specification of the service requirements down to the detailed Service Design.
    3.  The right-hand side of the V model focuses on the validation activities that are performed against the specifications defined on the left-hand side.
    4.  Customers who sign off the agreed service requirements will also sign off the Service Acceptance Criteria and test plan.
    a.  1 only
    b.  2 and 3 only
    c.  1, 2 and 3 only
    d.  All of the above

4.  Consider the following activities from the Change Management process:
    1.  Review the Change
    2.  Assess and evaluate the Change
    3.  Authorize the Change
    4.  Coordinate Change implementation
    5.  Review Request for Change
    Which of the following options describes the CORRECT order of the activities?
    a.  1, 2, 3, 4, 5
    b.  1, 3, 4, 2, 5
    c.  5, 3, 2, 4, 1
    d.  5, 2, 3, 4, 1

5.  Which of the following statements about the Configuration Management System are CORRECT?
    1.  It will hold details of all of the components of the IT infrastructure as well as the relationships between these components.
    2.  At the data level it consists of one and only one physical Configuration Management Database.
    3.  The Service Knowledge Management System includes the Configuration Management System.
    4.  It is maintained by Service Asset and Configuration Management.
    a.  1 only
    b.  2 and 3 only
    c.  1, 3 and 4 only
    d.  All of the above

# CHAPTER 6

# Service Operation

## 6.1 Lifecycle Phase

### 6.1.1 Introduction

*Goal*

The **goal** of Service Operation is to deliver and support services in an efficient and effective manner and to maintain stability in service operations while at the same time allowing for changes and improvement.

*Objectives*

The **objectives** of Service Operation are: coordinating and carrying out activities and processes required to provide and manage services for business users and customers within a specified agreed service level; Service Operation is also responsible for management of the technology required to provide and support the services.

*Scope*

Service Operation is about fulfilling all activities required to provide and support services. These include:

- the services
- the service management processes
- the technology
- the people

*Value to the business*

All stages in the service lifecycle provide **value to the business** but from a customer viewpoint, Service Operation is where the actual value is seen.

If the day-to-day operation of processes is not properly conducted, controlled and managed, then well-designed and well-implemented processes will be of little value. In addition there will be no service improvements if day-to-day activities to monitor performance, assess metrics and gather data are not systematically conducted during Service Operation.

## 6.1.2   Basic concepts

Service Operation is responsible for the fulfillment of processes that optimize the service costs and quality in the service management Lifecycle. As part of the organization, Service Operation must help ensure that the customer (business) achieves their goals. Additionally, it is responsible for the effective functioning of components supporting the service.

**Achieving balance** in Service Operation. Service Operation must try to achieve a balance between the following conflicting priorities:

- The view of IT as a set of IT services and the view of IT as a set of technological components (**external** view versus **internal** view).
- Achieving an IT organization in which **stability** and **response** are in balance. On the one hand, Service Operation must ensure that the IT infrastructure is stable and available. At the same time, Service Operation must recognize the business needs change and must embrace change as a normal activity.
- Achieving an optimal balance between **cost** and **quality**. This addresses IT's challenge to continually improve the quality of services while at the same time reducing or at the very least maintaining costs.
- Achieving a proper balance in **reactive** and **proactive** behavior. A reactive organization does nothing until an external stimulus forces it to act. A proactive organization always looks for new opportunities to improve the current situation. Usually, proactive behavior is viewed positively, because it enables the organization to keep a competitive advantage in a changing environment. An over-proactive attitude can be very costly, and can result in distracted staff.

It is very important that the Service Operation staff are involved in Service Design and Service Transition, and, if necessary, in Service Strategy. This will improve the continuity between business requirements, technology design and operation by ensuring that operational aspects have been given thorough consideration.

**Communication** is essential. IT teams and departments, as well as users, internal customers and Service Operation teams, have to communicate effectively with each other. Good communication can prevent problems.

## 6.1.3   Processes and other activities

This section briefly explains the processes and activities of Service Operation. There are some key Service Operation processes that must link together to provide an effective overall IT support structure. More information about each of these processes can be found in Section 6.2 of this study guide.

Service Operation processes:
- **Event management** - Surveys all events that occur in the IT infrastructure in order to monitor the regular performance, this can be automated to trace and escalate unforeseen circumstances.
- **Incident management** - Focuses on restoring failures of services as quickly as possible for customers, so that these have a minimal impact on the business.
- **Problem management** - Includes all activities needed for a diagnosis of the underlying cause of incidents, and to determine a resolution for those problems.
- **Request fulfillment** - The process of dealing with service requests from the users, providing a request channel, information, and fulfillment of the request.
- **Access management** - The process of allowing authorized users' access to a service, while access of unauthorized users is prevented.

Service Operation activities:
- **Monitoring and control** - Based on a continual cycle of monitoring, reporting and undertaking action. This cycle is crucial to providing, supporting and improving services.
- **IT operations** - Fulfill the day-to-day operational activities that are needed to manage the IT infrastructure.
- There are a number of **operational activities** which ensure that the technology matches the service and process goals. For example *mainframe management, server management and support, network management, database management, directory services management, and middleware management.*
- **Facilities and data centre management** refers to management of the physical environment of IT operations, which are usually located in computing centers or computer rooms. Main components of facilities management are for example building management, equipment hosting, power management and shipping and receiving.

### 6.1.4 Organization

Service Operation has some logical functions (see also 6.2) that deal with service desk, Technical Management, IT Operations Management and Application Management:
- A **service desk** is the Single Point of Contact (SPOC) for users, dealing with all incidents, access requests and service requests. The primary purpose of the service desk is to restore "normal service" to users as quickly as possible.
- **Technical management** refers to the groups, departments or teams that provide technical expertise and overall management of the IT infrastructure. Technical management plays a dual role. It is the custodian of technical knowledge and

expertise related to managing the infrastructure. But it is also provides the actual resources so support the ITSM lifecycle.

- **IT operations management** executes the daily operational activities needed to manage the IT infrastructure, according to the performance standards defined during Service Design. IT operations management has two functions: IT operations control, which ensures that routine operational tasks are carried out, and facilities management, for the management of physical IT environment, usually data centers or computer rooms.
- **Application management** is responsible for managing applications in their lifecycle. Application management also plays an important role in the design, testing and improvement of applications that are part of IT services. One of the key decisions in application management is whether to buy an application that supports the required functionality, or whether to build the application according to the organization's requirements.

The key to effective ITSM is ensuring that there is clear accountability, and that roles are defined to carry out the practice of Service Operation.

### Service desk roles
The following roles are needed for the service desk:
- **service desk manager**
  - manages service desk activities
  - acts as escalation point for supervisors
  - takes on wider customer service role
  - reports to senior managers about any issue that could significantly impact the business
  - attends Change Advisory Board meetings
  - overall responsibility for processing incidents and service requests
- **service desk supervisor**
  - ensures that staffing and skill levels are maintained
  - is responsible for production of management reports
  - acts as escalation point for difficult calls
- **service desk analysts**
  - deliver first line support by accepting calls and processing the resulting incidents or service requests, using incident and request fulfillment processes
- **super users**
  - business users who act as liaison points between business and IT

*Technical management roles*
The following roles are needed for the technical management areas:
- **technical managers/team leaders**
  - responsible for leadership, control and decision-making
- **technical analysts/architects**
  - defining and maintaining knowledge on how systems are related and ensuring that dependencies are understood
- **technical operators**
  - performing day-to-day operational tasks.

*IT Operation management roles*
The following roles are needed for IT Operations management:
- **IT operations manager**
- **shift leader**
- **IT operations analysts**
- **IT operators**

*Application management roles*
Application management requires **application managers** and **team leaders**. They have overall responsibility for leadership, control and decision making for the applications team or department.
**Application analysts** and **architects** are responsible for matching business requirements to technical specifications.

*Event management roles*
It is unusual to appoint an 'event manager' but it is important that event management procedures are coordinated. The service desk is not typically involved in event management, but if events have been identified as incidents, the service desk will escalate them to the appropriate service operation teams.
**Technical and application management** play an important role in event management. For example, the teams will perform event management for the systems under their control.

*Incident management roles*
The **incident manager** is responsible for:
- driving the effectiveness and efficiency of the incident management process
- producing management information
- managing the work of incident support staff (first tier and second tier)

- monitoring the effectiveness of incident management and making recommendations for improvement
- managing major incidents
- developing and maintaining incident management systems and processes
- effectively managing incidents using first, second, and third tier support

*Request fulfillment roles*
Initial service request handling is done by the service desk and incident management staff. Actual fulfillment will be undertaken by the appropriate service operation team(s) or departments and/or external suppliers.

*Problem management roles*
One person (or, in larger organizations, a team) should be responsible for problem management. This **problem manager** is responsible for coordinating all problem management activities and is specifically responsible for:
- liaison with all problem resolution groups to accomplish quick solutions to problems within SLA targets
- ownership and protection of the Known Error Database
- formal closure of all problem records
- liaison with vendors and other parties to ensure compliance with contractual obligations
- managing, executing, documenting and planning all (follow-up) activities that relate to major problem reviews

*Access management roles*
Since access management is the execution of security and availability management, these two areas will be responsible for defining the appropriate roles. Although usually no access manager is appointed by an organization, it is important there should be one process for managing privileges and access. This process and the related policy are usually defined and maintained by information security management and executed by various service operation functions, such as the service desk, technical management and application management.

There are several ways to organize Service Operation functions, and each organization will come to its own decisions based on its size, geography, culture and business environment.

### 6.1.5   Methods, techniques and tools

An important requirement for Service Operation is an integrated IT service management technology (or toolset) with the following core functionality:
- self-help (e.g. FAQ's on a web interface)
- workflow or process management engine
- an integrated Configuration Management System (CMS)
- technology for detection, implementation and licenses
- remote control
- diagnostic utilities
- reporting capabilities
- dashboards
- integration with business service management

### 6.1.6   Implementation and operation

There are some general implementation guidelines for Service Operation:
- **Managing changes in Service Operation** - Service Operation staff must implement changes without negative impact on the stability of offered IT services.
- **Service Operation and project management** - There is a tendency not to use project management processes when they would in fact be appropriate. For example, major infrastructure upgrades, or the deployment of new procedures are significant tasks where project management can be used to improve control and manage costs and resources.
- **Determining and managing risks in Service Operation** - In a number of cases, it is necessary that risk evaluation is conducted swiftly, in order to take appropriate action. This is especially necessary for potential changes or known errors, but also in case of failures, projects, environmental risks, vendors, security risks and new clients that need support.
- **Operational staff in Service Design and Transition** - Service Operation staff should be particularly involved in the early stages of Service Design and Transition. This will ensure that the new services will actually work in practice and that they can be supported by Service Operation staff.
- **Planning and implementation of service management technologies** - There are several factors that organizations must plan before and during implementation of ITSM support tools, such as licenses, implementation, capacity checks and timing of technology/implementation.

For a successful Service Operation, several challenges need to be overcome, such as:
- Lack of involvement among development and project staff.
- Justifying the financing.

- Challenges for service operation managers, for example ineffective Service Transition may hamper the transition from design to production, the use of virtual teams, and the balance between the many internal and external relationships.

There are some critical success factors:
- management support
- defining champions
- business support
- hiring and retaining staff
- service management training
- appropriate tools
- test validity
- measuring and reporting

Risks to successful Service Operation include:
- insufficient financing and resources
- loss of momentum in implementation Service Operation
- loss of important staff
- resistance to change
- lack of management support
- suspicion of service management by both IT and the business
- changing expectations of the customer

## 6.2 Functions and Processes

### 6.2.1 Event Management

*Introduction*
An **event** is defined as "any detectable or discernible occurrence that has significance for the management of the IT infrastructure or the delivery of IT service, and evaluation of the impact that a deviation might cause to the services."

Event management is the process that monitors all events that occur through the IT infrastructure to allow for normal operation and also to detect and escalate exceptional conditions. Event management can be automated to trace and escalate unforeseen event circumstances.

*Basic concepts*
Events may be classified as:
- **Events that indicate a normal operation** - For example a user logging on to use an application.
- **Events that indicate an abnormal operation** - For example a user who is trying to log on to an application with an incorrect password or a PC scan that reveals the installation of unauthorized software.
- **Events that signal an unusual but not exceptional operation** - It may provide an indication that the situation requires a little more supervision. For example utilization of a server's memory reaches within five per cent of its highest acceptable level.

Event management can be applied to any service management aspect that must be managed and can be automated.

*Activities*
The main activities of the event management process are:
1. **An event occurs** - Events occur all the time, but not all of them are detected or registered. Therefore, it is important to understand what event types must be detected.
2. **Event notification** - Most CIs are designed in such a way that they communicate specific information about themselves in one of the following ways:
   - A management tool probes a device and collects specific data (this is also called "polling").
   - The CI generates a report if certain conditions are met.

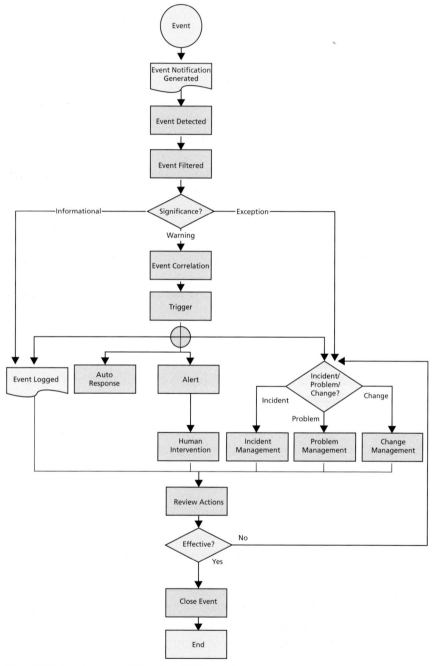

Figure 6.1 Event management (Based on: OGC source)

3. **Event detection** - A management tool or agent detects an event report and reads and interprets it.
4. **Event filtering** - Event filtering decides whether or not the event is communicated to a management tool.
5. The **significance of events** (**event classification**) - Organizations often use their own classification to establish the importance of an event. However, it is useful to use at least the following three broad categories:
   - informative
   - **alert** - an alert requires a person, or team, to perform a specific action, possibly on a specific device and possibly at a specific time. For example changing a toner cartridge in a printer when the level is low.
   - exception
6. **Event correlation** - Event correlation establishes the significance of an event and determines what actions should be taken.
7. **Trigger** - If the event is recognized, a response is required. The mechanism that initiates that response is called a trigger.
8. **Response options** - The process provides a number of response options, a combination of which are allowed:
   - event logging
   - automatic response
   - alert and human intervention
   - submitting a Request for Change (RFC)
   - opening an incident record
   - opening a link to a problem record
9. **Review actions** - All important events or exceptions should be checked to determine whether they have been treated correctly, or whether event types are counted.
10. **Closing the event** - Some events remain open until specific actions have been taken.

The diagram in Figure 6.1 reflects the flow of event management.

Each event type is able to trigger event management. Among other things, triggers include:
- Exceptions at every level of CI performance established in the design specifications, Operational Level Agreements or standard processing procedures.
- An exception in a business process that is monitored by event management.
- A status change that is found in a device or database record.

*Inputs and outputs*

Input:
- event notification

Outputs:
- incident record
- problem record
- Request for Change
- event record
- auto response
- alert and human intervention

## 6.2.2   Incident Management

*Introduction*

The incident management process handles all incidents. These may be failures, faults or bugs that are reported by users (generally via a call to the service desk) or technical staff, or that are automatically detected and reported by monitoring tools.

An **incident** can be defined as: "an unplanned interruption to an IT service or reduction in the quality of an IT service. Failure of a CI that has not yet affected service is also an incident."

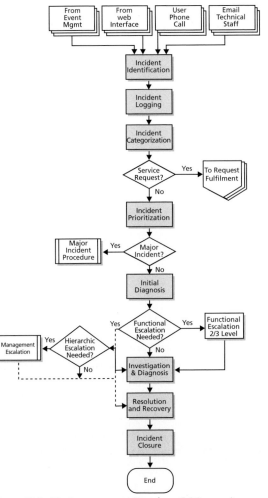

Figure 6.2 Incident management (Based on: OGC source)

*Basic concepts*
In incident management, the following elements should be taken into account:
- **Timescales** - Agree on time limits for all phases and use them as targets in Operational Level Agreements (OLAs) and Underpinning Contracts (UCs).
- **Incident models** - An incident model is a way of pre-defining the steps that are necessary to handle a process (in this case, the processing of certain incident types) in an agreed way. Usage of incident models helps to ensure that standard incidents will be handled correctly and within the agreed timeframes.
- **Impact** - The effect of an incident upon business processes.
- **Urgency** - A measure of how long it will be before the incident will have a significant impact on business processes.
- **Priority** - A category for the relative importance of an incident, based on impact and urgency.
- **Major incidents** - A major incident is an incident for which the degree of impact on the user community is extreme. Major incidents require a separate procedure, with shorter timeframes and higher urgency. Agree on what defines a major incident and map the entire incident priority system.

People sometimes confuse a major incident with a problem. However, an incident always remains an incident. Its impact or priority may increase, but it never becomes a problem. A problem is the underlying cause of one or more incidents and always remains a separate entity.

*Activities*
The incident management process consists of the following steps (Figure 6.2):
1. **Identification** - The incident is detected or reported.
2. **Registration** - An incident record is created.
3. **Categorization** - The incident is coded by type, status, impact, urgency, SLA, et cetera.
4. **Prioritization** - Every incident gets an appropriate prioritization code to determine how the incident is handled by support tools and support staff.
5. **Diagnosis** - A diagnose is carried out to try to discover the full symptoms of the incident.
6. **Escalation** - When the service desk cannot resolve the incident itself, the incident is escalated for further support (functional escalation). If incidents are more serious, the appropriate IT managers must be notified (hierarchic escalation).
7. **Investigation and diagnosis** - If there is no known solution, the incident is investigated.

8.  **Resolution and recovery** - Once the solution has been found, the issue can be resolved.
9.  **Incident closure** - The service desk should check that the incident is fully resolved and that the user is satisfied with the solution and the incident can be closed.

*Inputs and outputs*

Inputs:

- Incidents can be triggered in many ways. The most common route is via a user who calls the service desk or completes an incident registration form in a tool or via the internet. However, many incidents are registered by event management tools more and more often.

Outputs:

- incident management reports
- RFC
- workarounds
- problem reports
- service level reports
- requests

## 6.2.3   Request Fulfillment

*Introduction*
The term **service request** is used as a general description for the various requests that users submit to the IT department. A service request is a request from a user for information, advice, a standard change, or access to a service.

For example, a service request can be a request for a password change or the additional installation of a software application on a certain work station. Because these requests occur on a regular basis and involve little risk, it is better that they are handled in a separate process. Request fulfillment (implementation of requests) processes service requests from the users.

*Basic concepts*
Many service requests recur on a regular basis. This is why a process flow can be devised in advance, stipulating the phases needed to handle the requests, the individuals or support groups, time limits and escalation paths involved. The service request is usually handled as a standard change.

*Activities*
Request fulfillment consists of the following activities, methods and techniques:
- **Menu selection** - By means of request fulfillment, users can submit their own service request via a link to service management tools.
- **Financial authorization** - Most service requests have financial implications; the cost for handling a request must first be determined; it is possible to agree on fixed prices for standard requests and give instant authorization for these requests; in all other cases the cost must first be estimated, after which the user must give permission.
- **Fulfillment** - The actual fulfillment activity depends on the nature of the service request. The service desk can handle simple requests, whereas others must be forwarded to specialist groups or suppliers.
- **Closure** - Once the service request has been completed, the service desk will close off the request.

*Inputs and outputs*

Inputs:

- service requests
- Request for Change
- service portfolio
- security policies

Output:

- a fulfilled service request

## 6.2.4   Problem Management

*Introduction*
A **problem** is defined as: "the unknown cause of one or more incidents."

Problem management is responsible for the control of the lifecycle of all problems. The primary objective of problem management is to prevent problems and incidents, eliminate repeating incidents, and minimize the impact of incidents that cannot be prevented.

*Basic concepts*
A **root cause** of an incident is the fault in the service component that made the incident occur.

A **workaround** is a way of reducing or eliminating the impact of an incident or problem for which a full resolution is not yet available.

A **known error** is a problem that has a documented root cause and a workaround.

In addition to creating a **Known Error Database (KEDB)** for faster diagnosis, the creation of a problem model for the handling of future problems may be useful. This standard model supports the steps that need to be taken, the responsibilities of people involved and the necessary timescales.

*Activities*
Problem management (Figure 6.3) consists of two important processes:
• **Reactive problem management** - Analyzing and resolving the causes of incidents. Reactive problem management is performed by Service Operation.
• **Proactive problem management** - Activities to detect and prevent future problems/ incidents. Proactive problem management includes the identification of trends or potential weaknesses. It is initiated by Service Operation, but usually driven by CSI (see also Chapter 7).

*Inputs and outputs*
Inputs:
• problem records
• incident details
• configuration details from the configuration management database
• supplier details about the products used in the infrastructure

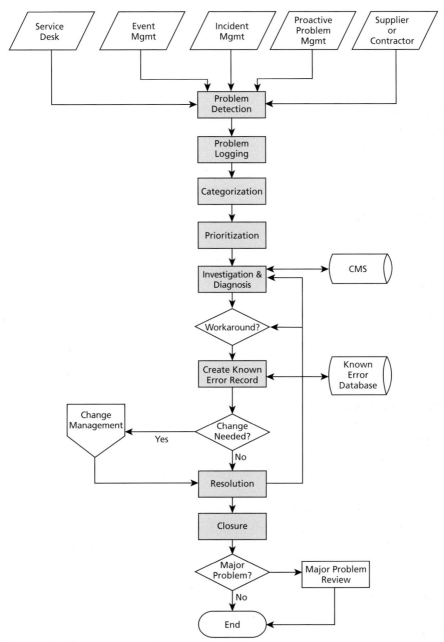

Figure 6.3 Problem management (Based on: OGC source)

- Service catalogue and service level agreements
- Details about the infrastructure and the way it behaves, such as capacity records, performance measurements, service level reports, et cetera.

Outputs:
- problem records
- Known Error Database
- Request for Change
- closed problem records
- management information

## 6.2.5   Access Management

*Introduction*
Access management grants authorized users the right to use a service, and denies unauthorized users access. Some organizations also call it "rights management" or "identity management".

Access management can be initiated via a number of mechanisms, for example by means of a **service request** with the service desk.

*Basic concepts*
Access management has the following basic concepts:
- **Access** - Refers to the level and scope of the functionality of services or data that a user is allowed to use.
- **Identity** - Refers to the information about the people who the organization distinguishes as individuals; establishes their status in the organization.
- **Rights** - Rights are also called privileges. Refers to the actual settings for a user; the service (group) they are allowed to use. Typical rights include reading, writing, executing, editing and deleting.
- **Services or service groups** - Most users have access to multiple services; it is therefore more effective to grant every user or group of users access to an entire series of services that they are allowed to use simultaneously.
- **Directory services** - Refers to a specific type of tool used to manage access and rights.

*Activities*
Access management consists of the following activities:
- **Requesting access** - Access (or limitation of access) can be requested via a number of mechanisms, such as a standard request generated by the human resources department; a Request for Change (RFC), an RFC submitted via the request fulfillment process, execution of an authorized script or option.
- **Verification** - Access management must verify every access request for an IT service from two perspectives:
  - Are the users requesting access, really the person they say they are?
  - Does the user have a legitimate reason to use the service?
- **Granting rights** - Give verified users access to IT services. Access management does not decide who gets access to what IT services; it only executes the policy and rules defined by Service Strategy and Service Design.

- **Monitoring identity status** - User roles may vary over time. Changes like job changes, promotion, dismissal, retirement all influence their service needs.
- **Registering and monitoring access** - Access management does not only respond to requests; it must also ensure that the rights it has granted are used correctly.
- **Logging and tracking access** - This is why access monitoring and control must be included in the monitoring activities of all technical and application management functions as well as in all the Service Operation processes.
- **Revoking or limiting rights** - In addition to granting rights to use a service, access management is also responsible for withdrawing those rights; but it cannot make the actual decision.

*Inputs and outputs*

Inputs:
- Request for change
- service request
- request from the Human Resources (HR) department
- request from a manager or department fulfilling an HR role or who has made a decision to use a service for the first time

Outputs:
- instances of access granted by service, user, department, et cetera
- reporting on abuses of user authorizations

### 6.2.6   Monitoring and Control

*Introduction*
The measuring and control of services is based on a continuous cycle of monitoring, reporting and initiating action. This cycle is essential to the supply, support and improvement of services and also provides a basis for setting strategy, designing and testing services, and achieving meaningful improvement.

*Basic concepts*
Three terms play a leading role in monitoring and control:
- **Monitoring** - Refers to the observation of a situation to discover changes that occur over time.
- **Reporting** - Refers to the analysis, production and distribution of the outputs of the activity that is being monitored.
- **Control** - Refers to the management of the usefulness or behavior of a device, system or service. There are three conditions:
    - The action must ensure that the behavior conforms to a defined standard or norm.
    - The conditions leading to the action must be defined, understood and confirmed.
    - The action must be defined, approved and suitable for these conditions.

There are two levels of monitoring:
- **Internal monitoring and control** - Focuses on activities and items exist within a team or department. For instance a service desk manager may monitor the number of calls to determine how many members of staff are needed to answer the telephone.
- **External monitoring and control** - Although each team or department is responsible for managing its own area, they do not act independently. Each team or department will also be controlling items and activities on behalf of other groups, processes or functions. For example, the server management team monitors the CPU performance on important servers and keeps the workload under control. This allows essential applications to perform within the target values set by application management.

*Activities*
The best-known model for the description of control is the monitoring/control cycle. Although it is a simple model, it has many complex applications in IT service management. Figure 6.4 reflects the basic principles of control.

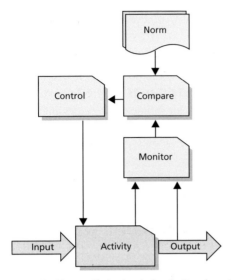

Figure 6.4 The monitoring/control cycle (Based on: OGC source)

The monitoring/control cycle concept can be used to manage:
- The performance of activities in a process or procedure.
- The effectiveness of the process or procedure as a whole.
- The performance of a device or a series of devices.

There are different types of monitoring tools, whereby the situation determines which type of monitoring is used:
- Active versus passive monitoring
- Reactive versus proactive monitoring
- Continuous measuring versus exception-based measuring
- Performance versus outputs

*Inputs and outputs*
ITIL does not define the inputs/outputs for monitoring and control in detail. In general, anything could be monitored. However, the main issue here is the definition of monitoring and control objectives. The definition of monitoring and control objectives should ideally start with the definition of the Service Level Requirements documents. The Service Design process will help to identify the inputs for defining operational monitoring and control norms and mechanisms.

Monitoring without control is irrelevant and ineffective. Monitoring must always be aimed at achieving the service and operational objectives. Therefore, if there is no clear reason for the monitoring of a system or service, there should be no monitoring.

### 6.2.7   IT Operations

*Introduction*
To focus on delivering the service as agreed with the customer, the service provider will first have to manage the technical infrastructure that is used to deliver the services. Even when no new customers are added and no new services have to be introduced, no incidents occur in existing services, and no changes have to be made in existing services - the IT organization will be busy with a range of Service Operations. These activities focus on actually delivering the agreed service as agreed.

*Basic concepts*
The **operations bridge** is a central point of coordination that manages various events and routine operational activities, and reports on the status or performance of technological components.

An operations bridge brings together all vital observation points in the IT infrastructure so that they can be monitored and managed with minimum effort in a central location.

The operations bridge combines many activities, such as console management, event handling, first line network management, and support outside office hours. In some organizations, the service desk is part of the operations bridge.

*Activities*
**Job scheduling**: IT operations execute standard routines, queries or reports that technical and application management teams have handed over as part of the service or as part of daily routine maintenance tasks.

**Backup and restore**: Essentially, backup and restore is a component of good continuity planning. Service Design must therefore ensure that there are proper backup strategies for every service. Service Transition must ensure that they are properly tested. An organization must protect its data, which includes backup and storage of data in reserved protected (and if necessary, accessible) locations.

A complete backup strategy must be agreed with the business and must cover the following elements:
- What data should the backup include, and how often must it be made?
- How many generations of data must be retained?
- The backup type and the checkpoints that are used.
- The locations used for storage and the rotation schedule.

- Transport methods that are used.
- Required tests that are used.
- Planned recovery point; the point to which data must be recovered after an IT service resumes.
- Planned recovery time; the maximum allowed time to resume an IT service after an interruption.
- How will it be checked that the backups are functional when they need to be restored?

In all cases, the IT operations staff must be qualified in backup and restore procedures. These procedures must be documented properly in the procedure manual of IT operations. Where necessary, you should include specific requirements or targets in OLAs or UCs, and specify user or customer obligations and activities in the relevant SLA.

A **restore** can be initiated from several sources, varying from an event indicating data corruption to a service request from a user or customer. A restore may be necessary in case of:

- corrupt data
- lost data
- a disaster recovery plan / IT service continuity situation
- historical data required for forensic investigation

Many services provide their information in **print** or electronic form (**output**). The service provider must ensure that the information ends up in the right place, in the right way and in the right form. This often involves Information security.

Laws and regulations may play an important part in print and output. The archiving of important or sensitive data is particularly important.

Service providers are generally deemed to be responsible for maintaining the infrastructure to make the print and output available to the customer (printers, storage). In this case, that task must be set in the SLA.

*Inputs and outputs*
Input:
- definitions of how to deliver the IT services as defined in Service Design and communicated in Service Transition

Output:
- IT services delivered to the customers

## 6.2.8   Service Desk

*Introduction*
A service desk is a functional unit with staff involved in differing service events. These service events come in by phone, internet or infrastructure, events which are reported automatically.

The service desk is a vitally important element of the IT department of an organization. It must be the only contact point, the Single Point of Contact (SPOC), for IT users and it deals with all incidents, access requests and service requests. The staff often uses software tools to record and manage all events.

*Basic concepts*
The primary purpose of the service desk is to restore "normal service" to users as quickly as possible. "Normal service" refers to what has been defined in the SLAs. This may be resolving a technical error, but also filling a service request or answering a question.

There are many ways to organize a service desk. The most important options are:
- **Local service desk** - The local service desk is located at or physically close to the users it is supporting.
- **Centralized service desk** - The number of service desks can be reduced by installing them at one single location.
- **Virtual service desk** - By using technology, specifically the internet, and by the use of support tools, it is possible to create the impression of a centralized service desk, whereas the associates are in fact spread out over a number of geographic or structural locations.
- **Follow-the-sun service** - Two or more service desks are located in different continents and combined in order to offer a 24/7 service.
- **Specialized service desk groups** - Incidents relating to a specific IT service may be routed straight to the specialized group.

*Activities*
Besides resuming normal service to the user as quickly as possible there are specific responsibilities for a service desk, for example:
- logging all incident/service request details
- providing first-line investigation and diagnosis
- resolving incidents/service request
- escalating incidents/service requests a service desk cannot resolve themselves within agreed timescales

- informing users about the progress
- closing all resolved incidents, requests and other calls
- updating the CMS under the direction and approval of Configuration Management if so agreed

In order to evaluate the performance of the service desk at regular time intervals, **metrics** must be established. This way, the maturity, efficiency, effectiveness and potentials can be established and the service desk actions improved.

Besides following "hard" metrics in the performance of the service desk, it is also important to carry out "soft" metrics: the Client and User Satisfaction Surveys (for example Do clients and users find that their phone calls are properly answered? Was the service desk associate friendly and professional?). Users can best complete this type of metrics, but specific questions about the service desk itself may also be asked.

*Inputs and outputs*
Inputs:
- incidents
- service requests

Outputs:
- investigation and diagnoses
- resolved incidents / service requests
- escalating incidents / service requests that cannot be resolved
- keeping users informed of progress
- closing resolved incidents, requests and other calls
- communication with users
- updating the CMS

## 6.3    Sample Questions

1. Which of the following statements BEST describes the objective of Service Operation?
   a. To design services to satisfy business objectives.
   b. To ensure that the service can be used in accordance with the requirements and constraints specified within the service requirements.
   c. To achieve effectiveness and efficiency in the delivery and support of services.
   d. To transform Service Management into a strategic asset.

2. Which of the following statements is the CORRECT definition of a Known Error?
   a. An action taken to repair the root cause of an Incident or Problem.
   b. A Problem that has a documented root cause or a Workaround.
   c. The unknown cause of one or more Incidents.
   d. A Problem that has a documented root cause and a Workaround.

3. Which of the following balances has to be dealt with by Service Operation?
   a. Supply versus demand
   b. Push versus pull
   c. Stability versus responsiveness
   d. Cost versus resources

4. Which of the following activities is NOT an activity in the Incident Management process?
   a. Incident Identification
   b. Incident Verification
   c. Incident Categorization
   d. Incident Prioritization

5. Which of the following activities is the Incident Manager responsible for?
   1. Producing management information.
   2. Monitoring the effectiveness of Incident Management and making recommendations for improvement.
   3. Managing the work for Incident support staff (first-line and second line).
   4. Managing major incidents.
   a. 1 only
   b. 2 and 3 only
   c. 1, 2 and 3 only
   d. All of the above

6. Which of the following is an objective for Problem Management.
   a. To define, document, agree, monitor, measure, report and review the level of IT service provided.
   b. To minimize the impact of Incidents that cannot be prevented.
   c. To restore normal Service Operation as quickly as possible and minimize the adverse impact on business operations.
   d. To act as a basis for automating routine Operations Management activities.

7. Which of the following are examples of Event types?
   1. Informational
   2. Warning
   3. Major
   4. Exception
   a. 2 only
   b. 2 and 3 only
   c. 1, 2 and 3 only
   d. All of the above

8. Which of the following options are typical ways of structuring and locating a Service Desk?
   1. Local Service Desk
   2. Centralized Service Desk
   3. Virtual Service Desk
   4. Follow-the-Sun
   a. 2 only
   b. 2 and 3 only
   c. 1, 2 and 3 only
   d. All of the above

9. Which of the following is NOT the responsibility of a Service Desk?
   a. Providing first-line investigation and diagnosis.
   b. Closing all resolved Incidents.
   c. Resolving those Incidents it is able to resolve.
   d. Closing all resolved Know Errors.

10. Which of the following is NOT described as a function but as a process in Service Operation?
    a. Event Management
    b. Applications Management
    c. IT operations Management
    d. Technical Management

# CHAPTER 7

# Continual Service Improvement (CSI)

## 7.1 Lifecycle Phase

### 7.1.1 Introduction

IT departments must continually improve their services in order to remain appealing to the business. This is placed within the lifecycle phase of Continual Service Improvement (CSI). In this phase, measuring and analyzing are essential in identifying the services that are profitable and those that need to improve.

CSI should be applied throughout the entire service lifecycle, in all phases from Service Strategy to Service Operation. This way, it becomes an inherent part of both developing and delivering IT services.

*Goal*
The main **goal** of CSI is the continual improvement of the effectiveness and efficiency of IT services, allowing them to better meet business requirements. This entails both achieving and surpassing the objectives (effectiveness), and obtaining these objectives at the lowest cost possible (efficiency). To increase the effectiveness you can, for instance, reduce the number of errors in a process. To make a process more efficient you can eliminate unnecessary activities or automate manual operations.

*Objectives*
The main **objectives** of CSI are:
- to measure and analyze service level achievements by comparing them to the requirements in the Service Level Agreement (SLA)
- to recommend improvements in all phases of the lifecycle
- to introduce activities which will increase the quality, efficiency, effectiveness and customer satisfaction of the services and the IT service management processes
- to operate more cost effective IT services without sacrificing customer satisfaction
- to use suitable quality management methods for improvement activities

*Scope*
The **scope** of CSI includes the following important areas:
- general quality of the IT management

- continual tuning of the IT services to the current and future needs of the business
- continual tuning of the IT service portfolio
- the maturity of the IT processes which enable the services

*Value to the business*
There are several reasons to monitor and measure:
- to **validate** previous decisions
- to set **direction** for activities in order to meet targets
- to **justify** (with facts) that a course of action is required
- to identify a point of **intervention** including required changes and corrective actions

CSI mainly measures and monitors the following matters:
- **Process compliance** - Are the new or modified processes being followed?
- **Quality** - Do the various process activities meet their goals?
- **Performance** - How efficient is the process?
- **Business value of a process** - Does the process make a difference?

### 7.1.2   Basic concepts
Organizational change is needed to make continual improvement a permanent part of the organizational culture. John P. Kotter, Professor of Leadership at the Harvard Business School, discovered eight crucial steps to successful organizational change:
- create a sense of urgency
- form a leading coalition
- create a vision
- communicate the vision
- empower others to act on the vision
- plan for and create quick wins
- consolidate improvements and create more change
- institutionalize the changes

In the 1980s, the American statistician Deming developed a step-by-step improvement approach: the **Plan-Do-Check-Act Cycle (PDCA)**:
- **Plan** - What needs to happen, who will do what and how?
- **Do** - Execute the planned activities.
- **Check** - Check whether the activities yield the desired result.
- **Act** - Adjust the plan in accordance to the checks.

These steps are followed by a consolidation phase to engrain the changes into the organization. The cycle is also known as the Deming Cycle (Figure 7.1).

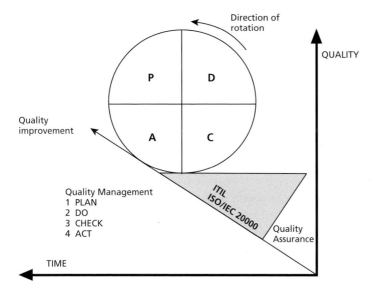

Figure 7.1 PDCA Cycle

CSI uses the PDCA Cycle in two areas:
- **Implementation of CSI** - Plan, implement (do), monitor, measure, and evaluate (check) and adjust (act) CSI.
- **Continual improvement of services and processes** - This area focuses on the "check" and "act" phase, with few activities in the "plan" and "do" phase, such as setting goals.

A **metric** measures whether a certain variable meets its set target. CSI needs three types:
- **Technology metrics** - Performance and availability of components and applications.
- **Process metrics** - Performance of service management processes.
- **Service metrics** - End service results, measured by component metrics.

Define **Critical Success Factors (CSFs)**: elements essential to achieving the business mission. **Key Performance Indicators** (KPIs) following from these CSFs determine the quality, performance, value, and process compliance. They can either be **qualitative** (e.g. customer satisfaction surveys), or **quantitative** (e.g. costs of a printer incident).

Metrics supply quantitative **data**. CSI transforms these into qualitative **information**. Combined with experience, context, interpretation and reflection this becomes **knowledge**. The CSI improvement process focuses on the acquirement of **wisdom**: being able to make the correct assessments and the correct decisions by using the data, information and knowledge in the best possible way. This is called the **data-information-knowledge-wisdom** model (DIKW).

Governance drives organizations and controls them. **Corporate governance** provides good, honest, transparent and responsible management of an organization. **Business governance** results in good company performances. Together they are known as **enterprise governance**. See Figure 7.2. **IT governance** is part of enterprise governance and comprises both corporate governance and business governance.

CSI policies capture agreements about measuring, reporting, CSFs, KPIs and evaluations.

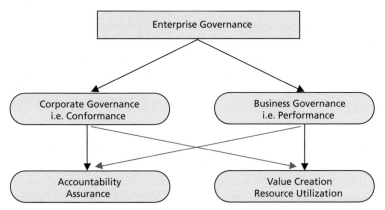

Figure 7.2 The enterprise governance framework (Source: CIMA)

### 7.1.3 Processes and other activities

This section briefly explains the processes and activities of Continual Service Improvement. More information about each of these processes can be found in Chapter 13 of this study guide.

Before you start with an improvement process, you should set the direction, using the CSI model:

1. **What is the vision?** - Formulate a vision, mission, goals and objectives together with the business.

2. **Where are we now?** - Record the current situation and set the baseline.
3. **Where do we want to be?** - Determine measurable targets.
4. **How do we get there?** - Draw up a detailed Service Improvement Plan (SIP).
5. **Did we get there?** - Measure whether the objectives have been achieved, and check whether the processes are complied with.
6. **How do we keep the momentum going?** - Engrain the changes in order to maintain them.

Continual Service Improvement processes:
- **The CSI improvement process** (or 7-step improvement process) - Describes how you should measure and report.
- **Service reporting** - Reports on results and service level developments.

Continual Service Improvement activities:
- **Service measurement** - Determines the value of the services with regard to the agreed service levels.

### 7.1.4 Organization

CSI comprises permanent production roles such as service manager, service owner, process owner and analysts, and temporary project roles such as project managers and project team members.

*Service manager*
The service manager manages the development, implementation, evaluation and ongoing management of new and existing products and services. The service manager is responsible for:
- achieving company strategy and goals
- benchmarking
- financial management
- customer management
- vendor management
- full lifecycle management
- inventory management.

The service manager must know a great deal about market analysis, be able to anticipate new market needs, formulate complex programs, guide personnel and sell services.

*CSI manager*

Without a clear and unambiguous responsibility, improvement will not occur. As a result this new role is essential for a successful improvement program. The CSI manager is responsible for CSI in the organization. The CSI manager manages the measuring, analysis, investigating and reporting of trends and initiates service improvement activities. In addition, the CSI manager also make sure that sufficient CSI supporting resources are available. The CSI manager is responsible for:

- development of the CSI domain
- awareness and communication of CSI throughout the organization
- allocating CSI roles
- identifying and prioritizing improvement opportunities to senior management together with the service owner
- identifying monitoring requirements together with the service level manager
- ensuring that the proper monitoring tools are installed
- creating SIPs together with the service level manager
- capturing baseline data to measure improvement against it
- defining and reporting upon CSFs, KPIs and activity metrics
- using supporting frameworks and models
- making knowledge management an integral part of the daily routine
- evaluating analyzed data.

The CSI manager must be able to lead projects throughout the organization, build good relationships with the business and IT management, have a flair for improvement opportunities throughout the company and be able to counsel staff.

*Service owner*

It is crucial to appoint one person responsible for each service: this is the service owner. The service owner is the central point of contact for a specific service. It does not matter where the underlying technological components, process or functions are located. The main responsibilities are:

- owning and representing the service
- understanding which components make up the service
- measuring the performance and availability
- attending **Change Advisory Board** (CAB) meetings if these changes are relevant to the service they represent
- working with the CSI manager to identify and prioritize improvements
- participating in internal and external service reviews
- maintaining the service entry in the service catalogue
- participating in the negotiation of SLAs and OLAs

*Process owner*

Having an owner is just as crucial to a process as a service owner is to a service. The process owner ensures that the organization follows a process. The service owner must be a senior manager with enough credibility, influence and authority in the organization departments which are part of the process. The process owner performs the essential role of process champion, design lead, advocate, coach and protector. See also chapter 4 "Service Design".

*Other roles*

Other roles that are important to CSI:

- **Service knowledge manager** - designs and maintains a knowledge management strategy and implements this.
- **Reporting analyst** - evaluates and analyzes data, and identifies trends; often cooperates with SLM roles (see Service Design); must have good communication skills because reporting is an essential element of communication.
- **Communication responsibility** - designs a communication strategy for CSI.

## 7.1.5   Methods, techniques and tools

There are various methods and techniques to check whether planned improvements actually produce measurable improvements:

- **Implementation review** - Evaluates whether the improvements produce the desired effects.
- **Assessment** - Compares the performance of a process or organization against a performance standard, such as an SLA or a maturity standard.
- **Benchmark** - A special type of assessment: organizations compare (parts of) their processes with the performance of the same types of processes that are commonly recognized as "best practice".
- **Gap analysis** - Determines where the organization is now and the size of the gap with where it wants to be.
- **Balanced Scorecard** - Includes four different perspectives on organizational performance: customer, internal processes, learning and growth and financial.
- **SWOT-analysis** - Looks at the Strengths, Weaknesses, Opportunities and Threats of an organization or component.
- **Rummler-Brache swim-lane diagram** - Visualizes the relationships between processes and organizations or departments with "swim lanes". Swim lanes are strong tools for communication with business managers, as they describe a process from an organizational viewpoint, and this is the way most managers look at a process.

In most cases, one method or technique is not enough: try to find the best mix for your organization.

CSI needs different types of software to support, test, monitor and report on the ITSM processes. The requirements for enhancing tools need to be established and documented in the answer to the question: 'Where do we want to be?'

### 7.1.6  Implementation and operation

Before you implement CSI you must establish:
- roles for trend analysis, reporting and decision-making
- a testing and reporting system with the appropriate technology
- services are evaluated internally before the IT organization discusses the test results with the business

The **business case** must clarify whether it is useful to start with CSI. On the basis of a set **baseline** an organization can compare the **benefits** and **costs** of the present situation with the benefits and costs of the improvement. Costs may be related to labor, training and tools.

Benefits of CSI may be:
- shorter time to market
- customer bonding
- lower maintenance costs

Critical success factors for CSI include:
- adoption by the whole organization, including the senior management
- clear criteria for the prioritization of improvement projects
- technology to support improvement activities

Introduction of CSI comes with the following challenges and risks:
- too little knowledge of the IT impact on the business and its important processes
- neglecting the information from reports
- insufficient resources, budget and time
- trying to change everything at once
- resistance against (cultural) changes
- poor supplier management
- lack of sufficient testing of all improvement aspects (people, process and products)

CSI uses a lot of data from the entire service lifecycle and virtually all its processes. CSI thus gains insight into the improvement opportunities of an organization.

**Service level management**, from the Design phase of the Lifecycle, is the most important process for CSI. It agrees with the business what the IT organization needs to measure and what the results should be. SLM maintains and improves the quality of IT services by constantly agreeing, monitoring and reporting on IT service levels.

As with all other changes in the Lifecycle, CSI changes must go through the change, release, and deployment process. CSI must therefore submit a **Request for Change** (RFC) with change management and conduct a **Post Implementation Review** (PIR) after implementation. The CMDB should be updated as well.

## 7.2   Functions and Processes

### 7.2.1   CSI Improvement Process

*Introduction*
The **CSI improvement process** or **7-step improvement process** describes how to
measure and report on service improvement. This process is closely aligned to the PDCA
Cycle and the CSI model, which should result in a **Service Improvement Plan (SIP)**.
Figure 7.3 shows how the CSI model and the CSI improvement process mesh together.

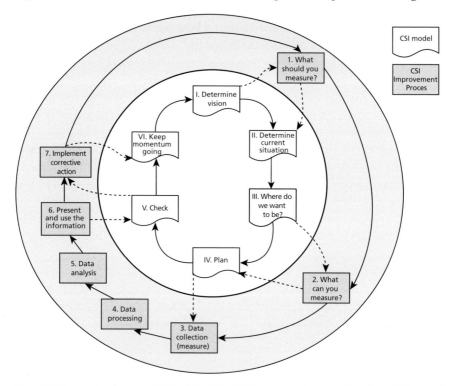

Figure 7.3 Connections between CSI Model and the CSI Improvement process (Based on: OGC source)

*Basic concepts*
**Measuring** is critical in CSI. It is step 3 of the CSI improvement process as discussed
below. It should, however, never become a goal unto itself. Always keep in mind *why*
you measure.

Before an organization can produce meaningful measurements, it needs to set its **baseline**, by answering the question "where are we now?". If there is little data available, first determine a baseline of relevant data.

Each management level should be addressed in the measuring process: strategic goals and objectives, tactical process maturity and operational metrics and KPIs. This way, a **knowledge spiral** develops: the information from Step 6 (Present and use the information) in an operational cycle is input for Step 3 (Data collection) in a tactical cycle, and information from Step 6 at the tactical level will provide data to Step 3 of a cycle at the strategic level.

*Activities*
CSI measures and processes measurements in a continual improvement process in seven steps:
1. **What should you measure?** - This must follow from the vision (Phase I of the CSI model) and precede the assessment of the current situation (Phase II of the CSI model).
2. **What can you measure?** - This step follows from Phase III of the CSI model: where do we want to be? By researching what the organization can measure, it will discover new business requirements and new IT options. By using a gap analysis CSI can find areas for improvement and plan these (Phase IV of the CSI model).
3. **Gather data (measure)** - In order to verify whether the organization has reached its goal (Phase V of the CSI model), it must perform measurements following from its vision, mission, goals and objectives.
4. **Process data** - The processing of data is to determine the right presentation format appropriate to each audience.
5. **Analyze data** - Discrepancies, trends and possible explanations are prepared for presentation to the business (Phase V of the CSI model).
6. **Present and use information** - The stakeholder is informed whether the goals have been achieved (still Phase V).
7. **Implement corrective action** - Create improvements, establish a new baseline and start the cycle from the top.

The cycle is preceded and closed by identification of vision and goals, which returns in Phase I of the CSI model: determine the vision.

*Inputs and outputs*
The inputs for the CSI improvement process going into Step 1 consist of:
- Service Level Requirements
- service catalogue
- vision, mission, goals and objectives of the organization and its units
- governance requirements
- budget
- balanced scorecard
- results from SIP coming from step 7

The *output* of Step 1 is a list of what should be measured, serving as *input* for Step 2. A list of what can be measured is the *output* of Step 2. These two lists provide input for Step 3, which creates the following *output*:
- monitoring plan and procedures
- collected data concerning the ability by IT to meet business expectations
- agreement on the reliability and applicability of data

Step 4 processes this into reports and logically grouped data ready for analysis as an *output* for Step 5. *Output* from step 5 is information turned into knowledge, according to the DIKW model. Step 6, must translate knowledge into wisdom which is required to make strategic, tactical and operational decisions.

The *inputs* for Step 7 are improvement opportunities suggested from Step 6. Step 7 assesses which opportunities provide the best possible outcome and implements those opportunities. This results into an SIP, which is the *output* of step 7. Measure whether desired improvements have delivered what you expected and use it as new *input* for Step 1.

## 7.2.2  Service Reporting

*Introduction*
The service reporting process reports on the results achieved and the developments in service levels. The aim is to convincingly support with facts any added value IT will have for the business. It should agree with the business on the layout, contents and frequency of the reports. Figure 7.4 shows how the service reporting process converts knowledge into the wisdom which is needed to make strategic, tactical and operational decisions.

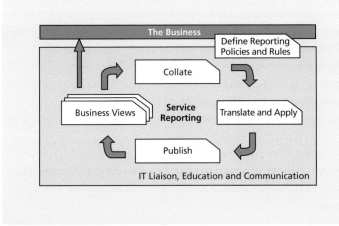

Figure 7.4 Service reporting (Based on: OGC source)

*Basic concepts*
A reporting framework is a policy that is formulated according to the rules by which you report. It should be established together with the business and Service Design, per business unit, so you can distinguish between, for example, production and sales departments. Once this has been determined, data can be translated automatically (if possible) into meaningful reports. The reporting framework should at least contain:
- target groups and their view of the services delivered
- agreement as to what should be measured and what to report
- defining all terms and upper and lower limits
- basis for all calculations
- report planning
- access to reports and media used
- meetings to discuss the reports

In order to provide useful reports to a customer, these reports should be set up from a business and end-to-end perspective. A customer is not interested in details about the functioning of the technical infrastructure through which services are provided, but only in the service itself.

### Activities
The service reporting process distinguishes the following activities:
- **Gather data** - First, determine the goal and target group of the report and consider how the report is going to be used.
- **Process and apply data** - Create a hierarchical overview of the performance over the past period, focusing on events that may impact the business performance. Describe how the IT department is going to combat those threats. Also describe what went well and how IT provides value to the business.
- **Publish the information** - Publish information for the different stakeholders at all levels of the organization. Use marketing and communication techniques to reach the different target groups such as the business and IT management.
- **Tune the reporting to the business** - Consider by data group if it is valuable for the target group. Look at this from an end-to-end perspective.

Evaluate continually whether the existing reporting provides clear and unambiguous information about the performance of the IT department and adjust your reporting, if this is no longer the case.

### Inputs and outputs
The *inputs* for the reporting process are the data gathered in step 3 of the CSI improvement process. It is important to determine what the *outputs* should look like well before the inputs arrives. IT departments frequently gather large amounts of data, which are not all equally interesting to the business. Start, therefore, by determining the goal and target group of the report and consider how the report is going to be used. Is management going to read it, can managers and department heads consult it online or are you going to present the results at a meeting? What will be done with it next?

Consider your audience. The organizational level of the target group will also influence its interest for different sorts of output:
1. **Strategic thinkers** - Strategic thinkers want short reports, with lots of attention to the risks, organization image, profitability and cost savings.
2. **Directors** - Directors want more detailed reports which summarize the development measured in time, indicating how processes support the company goals, and warning of risks.

3. **Managers and supervisors** - Managers and supervisors deal with observing the goals, team and process performance, distribution of resources and improvement initiatives. Measurements and reports must indicate how the process results are contributing to this.

4. **Team leaders and staff** - Team leaders and staff will look to emphasize the individual contribution to the company result; focus should be to fix individual metrics, acknowledge their skills and consider which training potential is available in order to involve them in the processes.

## 7.3 Sample Questions

1. Which of the following is NOT an activity in the Deming PDCA cycle?
   a. Plan
   a. Do
   b. Check
   c. Align

2. What are the reasons to monitor and measure?
   1. To validate - monitoring and measuring to validate previous decisions.
   2. To direct - monitoring and measuring to set direction for activities in order to meet set targets.
   3. To justify - monitoring and measuring to justify, with factual evidence of proof, that a course of action is required.
   4. To intervene - monitoring and measuring to identify a point of intervention, including subsequent changes and corrective actions.
   a. 1 only
   b. 1 and 2 only
   c. 1, 2 and 4 only
   d. All of the above

3. Which of the following is an objective for the 7-Step Improvement process?
   a. To provide operations visibility, insight and superior decision making.
   b. To design processes for the design, transition, operations and improvement of IT Services.
   c. To identify goals and objectives in order to properly identify what should be measured.
   d. To minimize the impact of Incidents that cannot be prevented.

# CHAPTER 8

# ITIL Foundation Exam

## 8.1 Prerequisites

There are no formal criteria or prerequisites for candidates wishing to take the ITIL Foundation Exam. However, candidates are recommended to attend an accredited training course. Candidates attending a training course are recommended to choose one of the accredited course providers (See chapter 1).

## 8.2 Format

The ITIL V3 Foundation Exam consists of 40 multiple choice questions. To pass the examination, 26 out of the 40 questions (65%) must be answered correctly. The duration of the examination is 60 minutes. Candidates sitting the examination in a language other than their native language have a maximum of 75 minutes and are allowed the use of a dictionary. It is not allowed to use books during the examination. The examination can be online or paper based. Candidates who fail may retake the examination, there is no limit to the number of times a candidate may retake the exam.

## 8.3 Exam Preparations

To make sure that you get the best possible mark in the examinations for the ITIL Foundation Certificate there are a couple of precautions you can take, the first one being to take the examination seriously.

### 8.3.1 Preparation for the exam

- Participate in an accredited training course. Learning the basics of IT service management is more fun and more effective if done in a group of professionals sharing experiences and with an experienced tutor with a depth of understanding and practical working experience.
- Plan to spend enough time for private study and revision of course materials, ITIL documentation and this training guide.
- Discuss what you learned in the training course and from the books with colleagues and friends. Sharing experiences about best practice helps you to understand IT service management principles.

### 8.3.2   Preparation for the day of the exam

- Plan your journey to the examination center. Aim to arrive fifteen minutes early to have a quiet start of the examination; for example, with a coffee or tea.
- Have a good night sleep and start the examination session well rested. Do not try to study the course material until deep into the night.
- Choose clothes that make you feel comfortable, you do not have to represent your company, you are representing yourself.
- Do not forget to bring a valid personal ID paper (passport, ID card).

### 8.3.3   Hints and tips during the exam

- Carefully read all the questions.
- In answering the multiple-choice questions, first try to think of an answer yourself before choosing one of the options. Your first hunch is often the best.
- Do not complicate the question by trying to find counter-examples for the answer you think is best. The questions are not meant to be tricky.
- Before the end of the examination sessions, check whether you have answered all the questions. If you are not sure, try your best choice.
- Do not spend too much time on any one question
- Do not panic. With the right kind of preparation, the examination is not very difficult, you can do it!

## 8.4   Sample Exam Questions

The following set of sample questions provides a good example of the kind of questions one may expect to find in the real examinations.

All 40 questions should be attempted.

There are no trick questions.

You have 60 minutes to complete this paper. Candidates sitting the examination in a language other than their native language have a maximum of 75 minutes and are allowed the use of a dictionary.

You must get 26 or more answers correct to pass. More sample papers can be requested from your course provider.

1   Which of the following statements BEST describes one of the purposes of Service Analytics?
   a.  Service Analytics is a means for automating simple and routine tasks and interactions.
   b.  Service Analytics is useful to restore normal Service Operation as quickly as possible in case of an incident.
   c.  Service Analytics is useful to model existing components and services to the higher-level business services.
   d.  Service Analytics is a means to ensure proper funding for the delivery and consumption for services.

2.  The goal of Problem Management is:
   a.  To prevent Problems and resulting incidents from happening.
   b.  To provide a channel for users to request standard services.
   c.  To restore normal Service Operation as quickly as possible.
   d.  To detect events, make sense of them, and determine the appropriate control action.

3.  Which of the following statements BEST describes the role of the Service Desk as the single point of contact?
   a.  All requests, such as incidents, Service Requests and Service Level Requirements form users and customers must pass through the Service Desk.
   b.  To provide a single point of contact to the users, an organization can only have one centralized Service Desk.
   c.  As a user I have one single point of contact for all incidents and Service Requests but other users in the organization may have other point of contact.
   d.  The Service Desk is on offer for the users in an organization. But they are of course allowed to contact anybody within the IT organization with their incidents and Service Requests.

4. Which of the following statements about the Process Owner role are CORRECT?
   1. Every person involved in a process is a Process Owner.
   2. The Process Owner is responsible for ensuring that the process is meeting the aims of the process definition.
   3. The Process Owner and Process Manager roles are always undertaken by the same person.
   4. Process Ownership is always a role as well as a function in any organization.
   a. 2 only
   b. 2 and 3 only
   c. 2, 3 and 4 only
   d. All of the above

5. Which of the following is NOT an activity in the Change Management process?
   a. Review the Request for Change
   b. Plan updates
   c. Change Design
   d. Assess and evaluate change

6. Which of the following are goals and objectives for the Service Level Management process?
   1. To provide and improve the relationship and communication with the business and customers.
   2. To produce and maintain an appropriate and up-to-date Capacity Plan which reflects the current and future needs of the business.
   3. To ensure that proactive measures to improve the levels of service delivered and implemented.
   4. To support efficient and effective business and Service Management processes by providing accurate information about assets.
   a. 1 only
   b. 1 and 3 only
   c. 1, 2 and 3 only
   d. All of the above

7. Which of the following metrics types is NOT a typical type of metrics?
   a. Technology metrics
   b. Service metrics
   c. Baseline metrics
   d. Process metrics

8.  Which of the following validation activities BEST corresponds to the definition of customer and business requirements (level 1) in the Service V-model?
    a.  Validate Service Package, offerings and contracts
    b.  Service operational readiness test
    c.  Service Release Package test
    d.  Component and assembly test

9.  Which of the following statements BEST describes the difference between an Operational Level Agreement and an Underpinning Contract?
    a.  Only the Operational Level Agreement is an underpinning agreement between an IT Service Provider and another part of the same organization that assists with the provision of services.
    b.  Only the Service Level Agreement defined the goods or services to be provided and the responsibilities of both parties.
    c.  Only the Underpinning Contract defines targets and responsibilities that are required to meet agreed Service Level Targets in a Service Level Agreement.
    d.  Only the Underpinning Contract support the IT Service Provider's delivery of IT services to customers.

10. Which of the following goals are the primary goals for Service Operations?
    1.  To allow for changes and improvement.
    2.  To design processes for the operation of IT services.
    3.  To achieve effectiveness and efficiency in the delivery and support of services.
    4.  To maintain stability.
    a.  3 only
    b.  3 and 4 only
    c.  1, 3 and 4 only
    d.  All the above

11. Which of the following is the CORRECT definition of Service Management?
    a.  Service Management is a set of specialized organizational resources for providing value to customers in the form of services.
    b.  Service Management is a set of specialized organizational resources for providing value to customers in the form of goods and products.
    c.  Service Management is a set of specialized organizational capabilities for providing value to customers in the form of services.
    d.  Service Management is a set of specialized organizational capabilities for providing value to the Service Provider in the form of goods and products.

12. Consider the following types of technological support of Service Management and the corresponding descriptions.
    A   Technology-assisted
    B   Technology-facilitated
    C   Technology-mediated
    D   Technology-generated (self-service)
    1.  The Service Provider is represented entirely by technology.
    2.  The Service Provider and the customer are not in physical proximity.
    3.  Only the Service Provider has access to the technology.
    4.  Both the Service Provider and the customer have access to the same technology.
    Which of the following pairings between roles and responsibilities is CORRECT?
    a.  A-3, B-1, C-2 and D-4
    b.  A-1, B-2, C-3 and D-4
    c.  A-3, B-4, C-2 and D-1
    d.  A-4, B-3, C-2 and D-1

13. Which of the following is NOT described as a function but as a process in the ITIL Service Management Practices framework?
    a.  Technical Management
    b.  Service Portfolio Management
    c.  Service Desk
    d.  Applications Management

14. Which of the following roles may be involved in the Continual Service Improvement process?
    1.  The Continual Service Improvement Manager
    2.  The customer
    3.  The Service Manager
    4.  The Process Owners
    a.  1 only
    b.  1 and 3 only
    c.  1, 3 and 4 only
    d.  All of the above

15. Which of the following statements BEST describes prioritization in the Incident Management process?
    a. Prioritization is determined by the urgency of the Incident and the level of impact the Incident is causing.
    b. Prioritization is determined by the resources available and the level of impact the Incident is causing.
    c. Prioritization is determined by the resources available and the urgency of the Incident.
    d. Prioritization is determined by the resources available, the urgency of the Incident and the level of impact the Incident is causing.

16. Which of the following questions is NOT one of the 7 Rs that must be answered for all changes as part of the impact assessment?
    a. What RESOURCES are required to deliver the change?
    b. Who RAISED the change?
    c. What is the RELATIONSHIP between this change and other changes?
    d. Who is going to REVIEW the change when it has been implemented?

17. The BEST way to define the services in the Service Portfolio is to base the definitions on:
    a. The resources needed to deliver the service.
    b. The business outcome of the service.
    c. The capabilities needed to deliver the service.
    d. The composition of the service.

18. Which of the following statements is the CORRECT description of the 'Act' stage in the Deming Cycle for quality improvement?
    a. At this stage goals and measures are established.
    b. At this stage the implemented improvements are compared to the measures of success.
    c. At this stage it is determined to keep the status quo, close the gap or add necessary resources.
    d. At this stage a project to close identified gaps is developed and implemented.

19. Which of the following questions helps identifying what a customer values?
    1. Who is our customer?
    2. Who depends on our services?
    3. How does the customer use our services?
    4. What do we provide?
    a. 1 only
    b. 1 and 3 only
    c. 1, 2 and 3 only
    d. All of the above

20. The goal of Continual Service Improvement is BEST described as:
    a. To continually align and re-align IT Services to the changing business needs by identifying and implementing improvements to IT services that support business processes.
    b. To encourage Service Providers to stop and think why something is to be done before thinking how.
    c. To continually identify and implement improvements to IT components that support the general technological developments.
    d. To design service that satisfy business objectives.

21. Which of the following are generic elements of a process?
    1. Process activities
    2. Process policy
    3. Process roles
    4. Process metrics
    a. 1 only
    b. 1 and 3 only
    c. 1, 2 and 3 only
    d. All of the above

22. Which of the following statements are CORRECT regarding the RACI authority matrix?
   1. The 'R' in RACI stands for 'Responsible'.
   2. The RACI chart shows the activities down the left-hand side and the functional roles across the top.
   3. More than one person can be accountable for each task.
   4. The 'I' in RACI stands for 'Initiator'.
   a. 1 only
   b. 1 and 2 only
   c. 1, 2 and 3 only
   d. All of the above

23. Which of the following is NOT an activity that IT Operations Management is responsible for?
   a. Console management
   b. Management of facilities
   c. Output management
   d. Maintenance of a stable technical infrastructure

24. Assume that IT Operations is separated from Technical and Application Management. Which of the following roles does Technical and Application Management normally NOT play in the Event Management process?
   a. Participating in the instrumentation of the service.
   b. Testing the services to ensure that Events are properly generated.
   c. Ensuring that any auto response are defined.
   d. Monitoring Events.

25. Which of the following statements are CORRECT about Service Asset and Configuration Management?
    1. Configuration Management delivers a logical model of the services, assets and the infrastructure.
    2. Information about each Configuration items is recorded in a configuration record in the Configuration Management System.
    3. The Service Knowledge Management System includes the Configuration Management System and databases as well as other tools and databases.
    4. Status Accounting and Reporting is an activity in the Service Asset and Configuration Management Process.
    a. 1 only
    b. 1 and 2 only
    c. 1, 2 and 3 only
    d. All of the above

26. Which of the following statements BEST describes the goals of Supplier Management?
    1. To ensure that underpinning contracts and agreements with suppliers are aligned to business needs and managed though their lifecycle.
    2. To manage relationships with suppliers.
    3. To ensure that the information security risks are appropriately managed and enterprise information resources are used responsibly.
    4. To maintain a supplier policy and a supporting Supplier and Contract Database.
    a. 1 only
    b. 1 and 2 only
    c. 1, 2 and 3 only
    d. All of the above

27. Which of the following activities BEST help an organization managing and developing Service Management as a strategic asset?
    1  Identification of critical services across the Service Portfolio for a given customer of market space.
    2. Establishment of the right mix of service to offer to customers.
    3. Tagging all service assets with the name of the service to which they add service potential.
    4  Creation of diagnostic scripts for diagnosis of incidents.
    a. 1 only
    b. 1 and 2 only
    c. 1, 2 and 3 only
    d. All the above

28. A key role for Service Operations is to achieve a balance between conflicting sets of priorities. A fundamental conflict exits between IT as a set of technology components on one side and:
    a. the view in which the organization focuses only on business requirements and the service delivered
    b. the ability to respond to change without impacting on other services
    c. a strong focus on delivering quality
    d. proactive behaviour on the other side

29. When should a Service Design Package be produced?
    a. During the strategy stage, for each time a new service is added to the Service Portfolio.
    b. During the design stage, for each change to a service or removal of a service.
    c. When a new or changed service is passed from Service Design to Service Transition.
    d. During the design stage, for each new service, major change to a service or removal of a service.

30. Which of the following benefits is NOT primarily the result of good Service Design practises?
    a. Reduced total costs of ownership.
    b. More effective Service Management processes.
    c. Increased success rate of changes and releases for the business.
    d. Improve quality and consistency of service.

31. ITIL is BEST characterized as:
    a.  An international standard
    b.  Good practise
    c.  A qualification scheme
    d.  Academic research

32. Which of the following activities is the Service Owner of a specific service responsible for?
    1.  Representing the service in Change Advisory Board meetings.
    2.  Participating in negotiating Service Level Agreements.
    3.  Defining the process strategy.
    4.  Liaising with the appropriate Process Owners.
    a.  1 only
    b.  1 and 2 only
    c.  1, 2 and 4 only
    d.  All of the above

33. Which of the following is the CORRECT order of the activities in the 7-Step Improvement Process (first activity first)?
    a.  1- Define what you should measure. 2- Define what you can measure. 3-Gather data. 4- Process data. 5- Analyse data. 6- Present information. 7-Implement corrective action.
    b.  1- Define what you can measure. 2- Define what you should measure. 3- Gather data. 4- Analyse data. 5- Process data. 6- Present information. 7- implement corrective action.
    c.  1- Define what you should measure. 2- Define what you can measure. 3-Gather data. 4- Analyse data. 5- Process data. 6- Present information. 7- Implement corrective action.
    d.  1- Define what you can measure. 2- Define what you should measure. 3- Gather data. 4- Process data. 5- Analyse data. 6- Present information. 7- Implement corrective action.

34. Which of the following methods is NOT a development approach?
    a.  Big-bang
    b.  Phased
    c.  Pull
    d.  Request

35. Which of the following activities forms part of the Service Portfolio Management process?
    1. Analyse
    2. Define
    3. Approve
    4. Charter
    a. 1 only
    b. 1 and 2 only
    c. 1, 2 and 3 only
    d. All of the above

36. To answer the question: 'Where do we want to be?' In the Continual Service Improvement model, we need to know:
    1. The vision of the organization
    2. The mission of the business
    3. The current baseline
    4. The metrics
    a. 1 only
    b. 1 and 2 only
    c. 1, 2 and 3 only
    d. All of the above

37. Good Service Design is dependent on effective and efficient use of the four Ps - people, processes, partners and:
    a. plans
    b. products
    c. practices
    d. policies

38. Which is the best description of a Service Catalogue?
    a. A document defining all aspects of an IT Service and its requirements through each stage of its lifecycle.
    b. The complete set of services that are managed by a Service Provider.
    c. A database or structured document with information about all live IT services, including those available for deployment.
    d. An agreement between and IT Service Provider and the IT customer(s).

39. Which of the following statements are CORRECT about utility and warranty?
    1. Utility can be described as what the customer gets.
    2. Warranty can be defined as 'fitness for use'.
    3. Utility increases the average performance.
    4. Warranty reduces the variation in performance
    a. 1 only
    b. 1 and 2 only
    c. 1, 2, and 3 only
    d. All of the above

40. The Service Portfolio is the single integrated source of information on the status, interfaces and dependencies of each service used by activities within the following stages in the Service Lifecycle:
    1. Service Strategy
    2. Service Transition
    3. Service Design
    4. Service Operation
    a. 1 only
    b. 1 and 2 only
    c. 1, 2 and 3 only
    d. All of the above

# Answers to the Sample Questions

## 2.6    Answers
1. c - Options (a), (b) and (d) are all stages of the lifecycle. Two other lifecycle stages not mentioned in the question are 'Service Design' and 'Service Transition'.
2. b - Option (2) and (4) are requirements for the processes and roles and not the tool.
3. d - All these guidelines should be considered when applying automation.
4. c - Option 4 (it can be repeated and becomes manageable) is a characteristic of a process.
5. d - All the four options are process characteristics.

## 3.3    Answers
1. c - Risk analysis involves the identification and assessment of the level of the risks calculated from the assessed values of assets (4) and the assessed levels of threats to (1), and vulnerabilities of (2), those assets, whereas countermeasures (3) are put in place based on the identified risks.
2. c - Option (2) 'practice' is not by itself a determinant for value proposition.
3. d - All of the activities are part of the Service Strategy management process.
4. a - 'Service devaluation' is not an activity in the Financial Management process, whereas 'Service valuation' is.
5. c - Major Incident Management is not a method drawn on by Demand Management.

## 4.3    Answers
1. c - This is one of the objectives of Service Transition.
2. b - Option (a) is incorrect because a Service Provider can provide services internally (called a type I or II Service Provider). Option (c) is the definition of a Supplier, and option (d) is a responsibility for the Availability Manager.
3. c - Strategy design is part of the Service Strategy stage of the lifecycle.
4. c - Rightsourcing is a popular way of saying that you need to make the right mix of the sourcing approaches.
5. a - Option (b) is an activity from the Service Asset and Configuration Management process, option (c) is an activity from the Release and Deployment Management process and option (d) is an activity form the Incident Management process.
6. b - Option (a) is an example of an Incident Management metric, option (c) is an example of a metric to measure the efficiency and effectiveness of the Change Management process, and option (d) is an example of a Continual Service Improvement metric.

7.  d
8.  b - There is nothing in ITIL called Configuration Capacity Management.
9.  c - RACI is an acronym for 'Responsible', 'Accountable', 'Consulted' and 'Informed'.

## 5.3    Answers

1.  b - Option (a) is a benefit of Service Operation option, option (c) is a benefit of Service Design and option (d) is a benefit of Continual Service Improvement.
2.  c - Known Change is not a specific term in ITIL.
3.  d - All statements are correct.
4.  d - The full list of the activities in the Change Management process can be found in Section 5.2.2.
5.  c - At the data level, the Configuration Management System may take data from several physical Configuration Management Databases, which together constitute a federated Configuration Management Database.

## 6.3    Answers

1.  c - Option (a) is an objective of Service Design, option (b) is an objective of Service Transition and option (d) is an objective of Service Strategy.
2.  d - Option (a) is the definition of a resolution, option (b) does not reflect that the definition of a Know Error requires both a root cause and a Workaround, and option (c) is the definition of a Problem.
3.  c - Options (a) and (d) are dealt with by Capacity Management in Service Design and option (b) refers to two alternative ways of deployment in Service Transition.
4.  b - Incident verification is not an activity in the Incident Management process.
5.  d - All the activities are part of the responsibilities of the Incident Manager.
6.  b - Option (a) is an objective for Service Level Management. Option (c) is an objective for Incident Management and option (d) is an objective for Event Management.
7.  c - 'Major' is not a type of Event but a 'type' of Incident.
8.  d - All of the options can be used to structure and locate a Service Desk. In reality, an organization may need to implement a structure that combines a number of these options to fully meet the business needs.
9.  d - Closing all resolved Know Errors is a responsibility of Problem Management.
10. a

## 7.3    Answers

1.  d - The activities in PDCA are Plan, Do, Check and Act.
2.  d - All the options are basic reasons to monitor and measure.
3.  c - Option (a) is an objective for Financial management. Option (b) is an objective for Service Design, and (d) is an objective for Problem Management.

## 8.4 Answers

1. c - Option (a) is an objective for Event Management. (b) is an objective for Incident Management and (d) is an objective for Financial Management.
2. a - Option (b) is a goal for Request Fulfillment, (c) is a goal for Incident Management and (d) is a goal for Event Management.
3. c - Single point of contact is seen from user's perspective. Option (a) is incorrect because customers requests such as Service Level Requirements normally go to a Business Relationship Manager, a Service Level Manager or similar. Option (b) is incorrect because different users can contact different Service Desks as long as each user has only one single contact point. Option (d) is incorrect because single point of contact is also a means to ensure that all users requests are logged and tracked by a dedicated function.
4. a - Only the person responsible for the process as a whole is the Process Owner; the Process Owner and Process Manager (i.e. Incident Manager) can be the same person, but is not necessarily the same person; and Process Ownership is always a role but is not necessarily implemented as a function in the organization.
5. c - There is no activity in the Change Management process for managing individual changes called 'Change Design'.
6. b - Option 2 is an objective for Capacity Management and option 4 is an objective for Service Asset and Configuration Management.
7. c - Baselines are markers or starting points for later comparisons of measurements.
8. a - Option (b) corresponds to level 3 (define Service Solution), option (c) corresponds to level 4 (define Service Release) and option (d) corresponds to level 5 (develop Service Solutions)
9. a - Option (b), (c) and (d) are true for both types of agreement.
10. c - Option 2, design of processes, is a goal for Service Design.
11. c - Service Management is a set of specialized organizational capabilities for providing value to customers in the form of services.
12. c
13. b - Service Portfolio Management is described as a process, whereas Technical Management, Service desk and Applications Management are described as functions in the Service Operation volume.
14. d - Not only all the internal roles in the Service provider organizations but also the customers should be involved in Continual Service Improvement.
15. a - The resources available are not determining the prioritization of the incident. Constraints to resources are the reason to do the prioritization.
16. d - The review and close of the change is not part of the impact assessment.

17. b - an outcome-based definition of services ensures that the organization plans and execute all aspects of Service management entirely from the perspective of what is valuable to the customer.

18. c - Option (a) is a description of the 'Plan' stage. Option (b) is a description of the 'Check' stage and option (d) is a description of the 'Do' stage.

19. c - Knowledge of the Service Provider's current services does not help identifying what a customer values.

20. a - Option (b) is the goal for Service Strategy, option (c) focuses on technological developments instead of the business needs and the supporting IT Services, and option (d) is an objective for Service Design.

21. d - All of the stated elements forms part of process as well as procedures, work instructions, triggers, input, output, capabilities, etc.

22. b - More than one person can be responsible for each task but only one person can be accountable for each task. 'I' stands for 'Informed'.

23. d - Technical Management, not IT Operations Management is responsible for planning, implementing and maintaining a stable technical infrastructure.

24. d - Where IT Operations is separated from Technical and Application Management, IT Operations is commonly delegated the Event monitoring and first-line response activities.

25. d - All of the statements are true, about Service Asset and Configuration Management.

26. c - Even though it is important to manage information security risks for data and services managed by third parties (option 3), this is a responsibility for the Information Security Management Process.

27. c - Options 1, 2 and 3 are all part of the activities involved in developing Service Management as a strategy asset within the Service Strategy Management process. Option 4 improves the Service Management processes but not necessarily as a strategic asset.

28. a - The other options are counterparts of stability, costs and relative behavior, respectively.

29. d - The Service Design Package should be produced during the design stage for new, changed and removed services. A Service Design package is normally only produced for major changes.

30. c - An increased rate of success of changes and releases is first and foremost a result of good Service Transition practices. The (a) total cost of ownership is reduced as a result of well-designed services, processes and technology, (b) more effective processes are a result of processes designed with optimal quality and cost effectiveness and (d) improved quality and consistency of services are the result of services designed within the corporate strategy, architecture and constraints.

31. b - ITIL is an example of good practice. (a) ISO/IEC 20000 provides a formal standard for organizations seeking to have their Service Management Capabilities audited and certified, (c) the IT Service Management certifications and diplomas owned by OGC and management by AMPG form an example of a qualifications scheme and (d) there are good examples of academic research supporting and/or criticizing ITIL itself is not academic research.
32. c - Defining the process strategy is a responsibility of the Process Owner, whereas the Service Owner is responsible for the three other activities.
33. a
34. d - A development method called 'Request' does not exist in ITIL. Option (a) is where the new or changed service is deployed to all user areas in one operation, (b) is where the service is deployed to a part of the user base initially and this operation is repeated for subsequent parts of the user base, and (c) is where the software is available in a central location but users are free to download the software at a time of their choosing.
35. d - All of the activities are part of the Service Portfolio Management process.
36. c - The answer to the question 'Where do we want to be?' Involves measurable targets, which are the prerequisites for defining the metrics. We therefore only need to know the vision, mission, goals, objectives and baseline to answer the question.
37. b - Good Service Design is dependent on all four answers, but the last 'P' in the four 'Ps' tenet stands for products.
38. c - The other are definitions of (a) a Service Design Package, (b) a Service Portfolio and (d) a Service Level Agreement.
39. d - All of the statements are true for utility and warranty.
40. d - The Service Portfolio acts as the connection point or the 'spine' of all five stages in the Service Lifecycle.

# Cross-reference to exam requirements

The following table shows a cross-reference to the official ITIL V3 exam requirements. The column to the right represents the section number in this guide were you can find the corresponding content. The requirements listed are taken from the syllabus: "The ITIL V3 Foundation Certificate Syllabus", Version 4.2.

| Unit | Requirements (with reference to ITIL core books) | Reference |
|---|---|---|
| ITILFND01 | **Service Management as a practice**<br>The purpose of this unit is to help the candidate to define Service and to and explain the concept of Service Management as a practice.<br>Specifically, candidates must be able to: | |
| 01-1. | Describe the concept of Good Practice (SS 1.2.2) | 2.1 |
| 01-2. | Define and explain the concept of a Service (SS 2.2.1) | 2.1 |
| 01-3. | Define and explain the concept of Service Management (SS 2.1) | 2.1 |
| 01-4. | Define Functions and Processes (SS 2.3, 2.6.1, SD 2.3, SD 3.6.4, SO 2.3, 3.1, CSI 2.3) | 2.5 |
| 01-5. | Explain the process model and the characteristics of processes (SD 2.3.2, 3.6.4) | 4.1<br>2.5 |
| The recommended study period for this unit is minimum 45 minutes | | |
| | | |
| ITILFND02 | **The Service Lifecycle**<br>The purpose of this unit is to help the candidate to understand the value of the Service Lifecycle, how the processes integrate with each other, throughout the Lifecycle and explain the objectives and business value for each phase in the Lifecycle.<br>Specifically, candidates must be able to: | |
| 02-2. | Describe the structure, scope, components and interfaces of the Service Lifecycle (SS 1.2.3 All) | 2.3 |
| 02-3. | Account for the main goals and objectives of Service Strategy (SS 1.3) | 3.1.1 |
| 02-4. | Account for the main goals and objectives of Service Design (SD 2.4.1, SD 3.1) | 4.1.1 |
| 02-5. | Briefly explain what value Service Design provides to the business (SD 2.4.3) | 4.1.1 |

| 02-6. | Account for the main goals and objectives of Service Transition (ST 2.4.1) | 5.1.1 |
| 02-7. | Briefly explain what value Service Transition provides to the business (ST 2.4.3) | 5.1.1 |
| 02-8. | Account for the main goals and objectives of Service Operations (SO 2.4.1) | 6.1.1 |
| 02-9. | Briefly explain what value Service Operation provides to the business (SO 2.4.3 1st para, SO 1.2.3.4) | 6.1.1 |
| 02-10. | Account for the main goals and objectives of Continual Service Improvement (CSI 2.4.1, 2.4.2) | 7.1.1 |

It is recommended that this training is covered within other units.
The recommended study period for this unit is minimum 1.0 hours.

| ITILFND03 | **Generic concepts and definitions**<br>The purpose of this unit is to help the candidate to define some of the key terminology and explain the key concepts of Service Management.<br>Specifically, candidates must be able to define and explain the following key concepts: | |
| 03-1. | Utility and Warranty (SS 2.2.2) | 3.1.2 |
| 03-2. | Resources, Capabilities and Assets (SS 3.2.1) | 3.1.2 |
| 03-3. | Service Portfolio (SS 4.2.3, SD 3.6.2 – to end of 1st bullet list) | 3.1.2 |
| 03-4. | Service Catalogue (Business Service Catalogue and Technical Service Catalogue) (SS 4.2.3.1, SD 4.1.4) | 3.2.2<br>4.2.1 |
| 03-5. | The role of IT Governance across the Service Lifecycle (CSI 3.10 All) | 7.1.2 |
| 03-6. | Business Case (SS 5.2.1 Intro, CSI 4.4.1) | 3.1.5<br>7.1.5 |
| 03-7. | Risk (SS 9.5.1, CSI 5.6.3) | 3.1.6 |
| 03-9. | Service Provider (the candidate is not expected to know the detail of each of the three types of Service Providers) (SS 3.3 Intro only, not 3.3.1, 3.3.2, 3.3.3) | 3.1.2 |
| 03-10. | Supplier (SD 4.2.4, 4.7.2) | 4.2.7 |
| 03-11. | Service Level Agreement (SLA) (SD 4.2.4, 4.2.5.1) | 4.2.2 |
| 03-12. | Operational Level Agreement (OLA) (SD 4.2.4) | 4.2.2 |
| 03-13. | Contract (SD 4.7.5.1) | 4.2.7 |
| 03-14. | Service Design Package (SD Appendix A) | 5.2.1 |
| 03-15. | Availability (SD 4.4.4) | 4.2.4 |
| 03-16. | Service Knowledge Management System (SKMS) (ST 4.7.4.2) | 5.2.7 |
| 03-17. | Configuration Item (CI) (ST 4.3.4.2) | 5.2.3 |
| 03-18. | Configuration Management System (ST 4.3.4.3) | 5.2.3 |

| 03-19. | Definitive Media Library (DML) (ST 4.3.4.3) | 5.2.3 |
| 03-20. | Service Change (ST 4.2.2) | 5.2.2 |
| 03-21. | Change types (Normal, Standard and Emergency) (ST 4.2.6.1, 4.2.4.5, 4.2.6.9) | 5.2.2 |
| 03-22. | Release Unit (ST 4.4.4.1) | 5.2.4 |
| 03-23. | Concept of Seven R's of Change Management (ST 4.2.6.4); no requirement to learn list | 5.2.2 |
| 03-24. | Event (SO 4.1 1st para) | 6.2.1 |
| 03-25. | Alert (SO Glossary) | 6.2.1 |
| 03-26. | Incident (SO 4.2) | 6.2.2 |
| 03-27. | Impact, Urgency and Priority (SO 4.2.5.4, 4.4.5.4) | 6.2.2 |
| 03-28. | Service Request (SO 4.3) | 6.2.3 |
| 03-29. | Problem (SO 4.4) | 6.2.4 |
| 03-30. | Workaround (SO 4.4.5.6) | 6.2.4 |
| 03-31. | Known Error (SO 4.4.5.7) | 6.2.4 |
| 03-32. | Known Error Data Base (KEDB) (SO 4.4.7.2) | 6.2.4 |
| 03-33. | The role of communication in Service Operation (SO 3.6) | 6.1.2 |
| 03-34. | Service Assets (SS 3.2) | 3.1.2 |
| 03-35. | Release policy (ST 4.1.4.2) | 5.2.1 |

It is recommended that this unit is covered as part of the training in the other units.
The recommended study period for this unit is minimum 1.0 hours.

| ITILFND04 | Key Principles and Models | |
| | The purpose of this unit is to help the candidate to comprehend and account for the key principles and models of Service Management and to balance some of the opposing forces within Service Management. Specifically, candidates must be able to: | |
| | **Service Strategy** | |
| 04-2. | Describe basics of Value Creation through Services (SS 3.1.1, 3.1.2) | 3.1.2 |
| | **Service Design** | |
| 04-3. | Understand the importance of People, Processes, Products and Partners for Service Management (SD 2.4.2) | 4.1.1 |
| 04-4. | Understand the five major aspects of Service Design (SD 2.4.2):<br>• Service Portfolio Design<br>• Identification of Business Requirements, definition of Service Requirements and design of Services<br>• Technology and architectural design<br>• Process design<br>• Measurement design | 4.1.2 |

| | Continual Service Improvement | |
|---|---|---|
| 04-8. | Explain the Plan, Do, Check and Act (PDCA) Model to control and manage quality (CSI 3.6, 5.5.1, Fig 5.6) | 7.1.2 |
| 04-9. | Explain the Continual Service Improvement Model (CSI 2.4.4, Fig 2.3) | 7.1.3 7.2.1 |
| 04-10. | Understand the role of measurement for Continual Service Improvement and explain the following key elements:<br>• The role of KPIs in the Improvement Process (CSI 4.1.2)<br>• Baselines (CSI 3.7.1)<br>• Types of metrics (technology metrics, process metrics, service metrics) (CSI 4.1.2) | 7.1.2 7.1.3 |
| The recommended study period for this unit is minimum 1.5 hours. | | |
| | | |
| ITILFND05 | Processes<br><br>The purpose of this unit is to help the candidate understand how the Service Management processes contribute to the Service Lifecycle, to explain the high level objectives, scope, basic concepts, activities and challenges for five of the core processes, and to state the objectives and some of the basic concepts for thirteen of the remaining processes including how they relate to each other.<br><br>The list of activities to be included from each process is the minimum required and should not be taken as an exhaustive list.<br><br>Specifically, candidates must be able to: | |
| | Service Strategy | |
| | State the objectives and basic concepts for: | |
| 05-21. | Demand Management (SS 5.5)<br>The following list must be covered:<br>• Challenges in managing demand for Services (SS 5.5.1)<br>• Activity-based Demand Management (Patterns of business activity (PBAs) (SS 5.5.2)<br>• Business activity patterns and user profiles (SS 5.5.3) | 3.2.3 |
| 05-22. | Financial Management (SS 5.1 Intro, 5.1.2 Intro)<br>• Business case | 3.2.1 3.1.5 |

| | Service Design | |
|---|---|---|
| | Explain the high level objectives, basic concepts, process activities and relationships for: | |
| 05-31. | Service Level Management (SLM) (SD 4.2.1, 4.2.2, 4.2.5, 4.2.5.1 - 9, CSI 3.5) <br> The following list must be covered: <br> • Service-based SLA <br> • Multi-level SLAs <br> • Service level requirements (SLRs) <br> • SLAM chart <br> • Service review <br> • Service improvement plan (SIP) | 4.2.2 <br> 7.2.1 |
| | State the objectives and basic concepts for: | |
| 05-41. | Service Catalogue Management (SD 4.1 Intro, 4.1.1, 4.1.4) | 4.2.1 |
| 05-42. | Availability Management (SD 4.4.1, 4.4.4) <br> • Service availability <br> • Component availability <br> • Reliability <br> • Maintainability <br> • Serviceability | 4.2.4 |
| 05-43. | Information Security Management (ISM) (SD 4.6 Intro, 4.6.1, 4.6.4) <br> • Security framework (SD 4.6.4.1) <br> • Information security policy (SD 4.6.4.2) <br> • Information security management system (ISMS) (SD 4.6.4.3) | 4.2.6 |
| 05-44. | Supplier Management (SD 4.7 Intro, 4.7.1) <br> • Supplier Contract Database (SCD) (SD 4.7.4) | 4.2.7 |
| 05-45. | Capacity Management (SD 4.3.1, 4.3.4) <br> • Capacity plan <br> • Business capacity management <br> • Service capacity management <br> • Component capacity management | 4.2.3 |
| 05-46. | IT Service Continuity Management (SD 4.5.1, 4.5.4) <br> • Business Continuity Plans <br> • Business Continuity Management <br> • Business Impact Analysis <br> • Risk Analysis | 4.2.5 |

| | Service Transition | |
|---|---|---|
| | Explain the high level objectives, basic concepts, process activities and relationships for: | |
| 05-51. | Change Management (ST 4.2)<br>• Types of change request (ST 4.2.4.3, Table 4.3)<br>• Change process models and workflows (ST 4.2.4.4)<br>• Standard change (ST 4.2.4.5)<br>• Remediation Planning (ST 4.2.5)<br>• Change Advisory Board / Emergency Change Advisory Board (ST 4.2.6.8) | 5.2.2 |
| 05-52. | Service Asset and Configuration Management (SACM) (ST 4.3.1, 4.3.4, 4.3.5) to include:<br>• The Configuration Model<br>• Configuration items<br>• Configuration Management System (CMS)<br>• Definitive Media Library<br>• Configuration baseline | 5.2.3 |
| | State the objectives and basic concepts for: | |
| 05-61. | Release and Deployment Management (ST 4.4.1, 4.4.4) | 5.2.4 |
| 05-62. | Knowledge Management (ST 4.7 Intro, 4.7.1, 4.7.4)<br>• DIKW & SKMS | 5.2.7 |
| | Service Operation | |
| | Explain the high level objectives, basic concepts, process activities and relationships for: | |
| 05-71. | Incident Management (SO 4.2, Fig 4.2) | 6.2.1 |
| 05-72. | Problem Management (SO 4.4, Fig 4.4), not PM techniques | 6.2.4 |
| | State the objectives and basic concepts for: | |
| 05-81. | Event Management (SO 4.1 Intro, 4.1.1, 4.1.4) | 6.2.1 |
| 05-82. | Request Fulfilments (SO 4.3 Intro, 4.3.1, 4.3.4) | 6.2.3 |
| 05-83. | Access Management (SO 4.5 Intro, 4.5.1, 4.5.4) | 6.2.5 |
| The recommended study period for this unit is minimum 10.0 hours. | | |
| | | |
| ITILFND06 | **Functions**<br>The purpose of this unit is to help the candidate to explain the role, objectivesorganizational structures of the Service Desk function, and to state the role, and overlap of three other functions.<br>Specifically, candidates must be able to: | |
| 06-1. | Explain the role, objectives and organizational structures for<br>• The Service Desk function (SO 6.2) | 6.1.4<br>6.2.8 |

| 06-2. | State the role, objectives and organizational overlap of: <br><br> • The Technical Management function (SO 6.1, 6.3 Intro, 6.3.1, 6.3.2) <br><br> • The Application Management function (SO 6.5 Intro, 6.5.1, 6.5.2) <br><br> • The IT Operations Management function (IT Operations Facilities Management) (SO 6.4 Intro, 6.4.1, 6.4.2) | 6.1.4 |
|---|---|---|
| The recommended study period for this unit is minimum 1.0 hours. | | |
| | | |
| **ITILFND07** | **Roles** <br> The purpose of this unit is to help the candidate to account for and to be aware of the responsibilities of some of the key roles in Service Management. <br> Specifically, candidates must be able to: | |
| 07-1. | Account for the role and the responsibilities of the <br><br> • Process owner (SD 6.4 Intro, 6.4.1) <br><br> • Service owner (CSI 6.1 Intro, 6.1.4) | 2.5 <br> 3.1.4 <br> 5.1.4 <br> 7.1.4 |
| 07-2. | Recognize the RACI model and explain its role in determining organizational structure. (SD 6 Intro, CSI 6.2 – not RASI-VS or RASCI) | 4.1.4 |
| The recommended study period for this unit is minimum 30 minutes. | | |
| | | |
| **ITILFND08** | **Technology and Architecture** <br> The purpose of this unit is to help the candidate to: | |
| 08-2. | Understand how Service Automation assists with integrating Service Management processes (SS 8.1) | 2.2 |
| It is recommended that this unit is covered as part of the training in the other units. | | |
| | | |
| **ITILFND09** | **ITIL V3 Qualification scheme** <br> The purpose of this unit is to help the candidate to: | |
| 09-1. | Explain the ITIL Qualification scheme, distinguish between the purposes of the two intermediate streams, mention the included certificates, ITIL Expert and ITIL Master, and understand the different options for further training. | 1.2 |
| The recommended study period for this unit is minimum 15 minutes. | | |
| | | |

| ITILFND10 | Mock exam | |
|---|---|---|
| | The purpose of this unit is to help the candidate to pass the ITIL Foundation Exam. | |
| | Specifically, candidates must: | |
| 10-1. | Sit minimum one ITIL Foundation mock exam. | 8.4 |
| The recommended study period for this unit is minimum 2.0 hours inclusive of revision. | | |

# Glossary

Where a term is relevant to a particular phase in the Lifecycle of an IT Service, or to one of the Core ITIL publications, this is indicated at the beginning of the definition. This glossary is based on the official ITIL V3 Glossary, version 01 of 30 May 2007.

| | |
|---|---|
| Acceptance | Formal agreement that an IT Service, Process, Plan, or other Deliverable is complete, accurate, Reliable and meets its specified Requirements. Acceptance is usually preceded by Evaluation or Testing and is often required before proceeding to the next stage of a Project or Process.<br>See Service Acceptance Criteria. |
| Access Management | (Service Operation) The Process responsible for allowing Users to make use of IT Services, data, or other Assets. Access Management helps to protect the Confidentiality, Integrity and Availability of Assets by ensuring that only authorized Users are able to access or modify the Assets. Access Management is sometimes referred to as Rights Management or Identity Management. |
| Account Manager | (Service Strategy) A Role that is very similar to Business Relationship Manager, but includes more commercial aspects. Most commonly used when dealing with External Customers. |
| Accounting | (Service Strategy) The Process responsible for identifying actual Costs of delivering IT Services, comparing these with budgeted costs, and managing variance from the Budget. |
| Accredited | Officially authorized to carry out a Role. For example an Accredited body may be authorized to provide training or to conduct Audits. |
| Active Monitoring | (Service Operation) Monitoring of a Configuration Item or an IT Service that uses automated regular checks to discover the current status.<br>See Passive Monitoring. |
| Activity | A set of actions designed to achieve a particular result. Activities are usually defined as part of Processes or Plans, and are documented in Procedures. |
| Agreed Service Time | (Service Design) A synonym for Service Hours, commonly used in formal calculations of Availability. See Downtime. |
| Agreement | A Document that describes a formal understanding between two or more parties. An Agreement is not legally binding, unless it forms part of a Contract.<br>See Service Level Agreement, Operational Level Agreement. |
| Alert | (Service Operation) A warning that a threshold has been reached, something has changed, or a Failure has occurred. Alerts are often created and managed by System Management tools and are managed by the Event Management Process. |

Analytical Modeling    (Service Strategy) (Service Design) (Continual Service Improvement) A technique
                       that uses mathematical Models to predict the behavior of a Configuration Item or
                       IT Service. Analytical Models are commonly used in Capacity Management and
                       Availability Management.
                       See Modeling.

Application            Software that provides Functions that are required by an IT Service. Each
                       Application may be part of more than one IT Service. An Application runs on one
                       or more Servers or Clients.
                       See Application Management, Application Portfolio.

Application            (Service Design) (Service Operation) The Function responsible for managing
Management             Applications throughout their Lifecycle.

Application Portfolio  (Service Design) A database or structured Document used to manage Applications
                       throughout their Lifecycle. The Application Portfolio contains key Attributes of all
                       Applications. The Application Portfolio is sometimes implemented as part of the
                       Service Portfolio, or as part of the Configuration Management System.

Application Service    (Service Design) An External Service Provider that provides IT Services using
Provider (ASP)         Applications running at the Service Provider's premises. Users access the
                       Applications by network connections to the Service Provider.

Application Sizing     (Service Design) The Activity responsible for understanding the Resource
                       Requirements needed to support a new Application, or a major Change to an
                       existing Application. Application Sizing helps to ensure that the IT Service can
                       meet its agreed Service Level Targets for Capacity and Performance.

Architecture           (Service Design) The structure of a System or IT Service, including the
                       Relationships of Components to each other and to the environment they are in.
                       Architecture also includes the Standards and Guidelines which guide the design
                       and evolution of the System.

Assembly               (Service Transition) A Configuration Item that is made up from a number of other
                       CIs. For example a Server CI may contain CIs for CPUs, Disks, Memory etc.; an IT
                       Service CI may contain many Hardware, Software and other CIs.
                       See Component CI, Build.

Assessment             Inspection and analysis to check whether a Standard or set of Guidelines is being
                       followed, that Records are accurate, or that Efficiency and Effectiveness targets are
                       being met.
                       See Audit.

Asset                  (Service Strategy) Any Resource or Capability. Assets of a Service Provider include
                       anything that could contribute to the delivery of a Service. Assets can be one of
                       the following types: Management, Organization, Process, Knowledge, People,
                       Information, Applications, Infrastructure, and Financial Capital.

| | |
|---|---|
| Asset Management | (Service Transition) Asset Management is the Process responsible for tracking and reporting the value and ownership of financial Assets throughout their Lifecycle. Asset Management is part of an overall Service Asset and Configuration Management Process.<br>See Asset Register. |
| Asset Register | (Service Transition) A list of Assets, which includes their ownership and value. The Asset Register is maintained by Asset Management. |
| Attribute | (Service Transition) A piece of information about a Configuration Item. Examples are name, location, Version number, and Cost. Attributes of CIs are recorded in the Configuration Management Database (CMDB).<br>See Relationship. |
| Audit | Formal inspection and verification to check whether a Standard or set of Guidelines is being followed, that Records are accurate, or that Efficiency and Effectiveness targets are being met. An Audit may be carried out by internal or external groups.<br>See Certification, Assessment. |
| Authority Matrix | Synonym for RACI. |
| Automatic Call Distribution (ACD) | (Service Operation) Use of Information Technology to direct an incoming telephone call to the most appropriate person in the shortest possible time. ACD is sometimes called Automated Call Distribution. |
| Availability | (Service Design) Ability of a Configuration Item or IT Service to perform its agreed Function when required. Availability is determined by Reliability, Maintainability, Serviceability, Performance, and Security. Availability is usually calculated as a percentage. This calculation is often based on Agreed Service Time and Downtime. It is Best Practice to calculate Availability using measurements of the Business output of the IT Service. |
| Availability Management | (Service Design) The Process responsible for defining, analyzing, Planning, measuring and improving all aspects of the Availability of IT Services. Availability Management is responsible for ensuring that all IT Infrastructure, Processes, Tools, Roles etc are appropriate for the agreed Service Level Targets for Availability. |
| Availability Management Information System (AMIS) | (Service Design) A virtual repository of all Availability Management data, usually stored in multiple physical locations.<br>See Service Knowledge Management System. |
| Availability Plan | (Service Design) A Plan to ensure that existing and future Availability Requirements for IT Services can be provided Cost Effectively. |
| Back-out | Synonym for Remediation. |
| Backup | (Service Design) (Service Operation) Copying data to protect against loss of Integrity or Availability of the original. |

Balanced Scorecard   (Continual Service Improvement) A management tool developed by Drs. Robert
Kaplan (Harvard Business School) and David Norton. A Balanced Scorecard
enables a Strategy to be broken down into Key Performance Indicators.
Performance against the KPIs is used to demonstrate how well the Strategy is
being achieved. A Balanced Scorecard has 4 major areas, each of which has a
small number of KPIs. The same 4 areas are considered at different levels of detail
throughout the Organization.

Baseline   (Continual Service Improvement) A Benchmark used as a reference point. For
example:
- An ITSM Baseline can be used as a starting point to measure the effect of a
  Service Improvement Plan
- A Performance Baseline can be used to measure changes in Performance over
  the lifetime of an IT Service
- A Configuration Management Baseline can be used to enable the IT
  Infrastructure to be restored to a known Configuration if a Change or Release
  fails

Benchmark   (Continual Service Improvement) The recorded state of something at a specific
point in time. A Benchmark can be created for a Configuration, a Process, or any
other set of data. For example, a benchmark can be used in:
- Continual Service Improvement, to establish the current state for managing
  improvements.
- Capacity Management, to document Performance characteristics during
  normal operations.
- See Benchmarking, Baseline.

Benchmarking   (Continual Service Improvement) Comparing a Benchmark with a Baseline or
with Best Practice. The term Benchmarking is also used to mean creating a series
of Benchmarks over time, and comparing the results to measure progress or
improvement.

Best Practice   Proven Activities or Processes that have been successfully used by multiple
Organizations. ITIL is an example of Best Practice.

Brainstorming   (Service Design) A technique that helps a team to generate ideas. Ideas are not
reviewed during the Brainstorming session, but at a later stage. Brainstorming is
often used by Problem Management to identify possible causes.

British Standards   The UK National Standards body, responsible for creating and maintaining British
Institution (BSI)   Standards. See http://www.bsi-global.com for more information.
See ISO.

Budget   A list of all the money an Organization or Business Unit plans to receive, and plans
to pay out, over a specified period of time.
See Budgeting, Planning.

| | |
|---|---|
| Budgeting | The Activity of predicting and controlling the spending of money. Consists of a periodic negotiation cycle to set future Budgets (usually annual) and the day-to-day monitoring and adjusting of current Budgets. |
| Build | (Service Transition) The Activity of assembling a number of Configuration Items to create part of an IT Service. The term Build is also used to refer to a Release that is authorized for distribution. For example Server Build or laptop Build. See Configuration Baseline. |
| Build Environment | (Service Transition) A controlled Environment where Applications, IT Services and other Builds are assembled prior to being moved into a Test or Live Environment. |
| Business | (Service Strategy) An overall corporate entity or Organization formed of a number of Business Units. In the context of ITSM, the term Business includes public sector and not-for-profit organizations, as well as companies. An IT Service Provider provides IT Services to a Customer within a Business. The IT Service Provider may be part of the same Business as their Customer (Internal Service Provider), or part of another Business (External Service Provider). |
| Business Capacity Management (BCM) | (Service Design) In the context of ITSM, Business Capacity Management is the Activity responsible for understanding future Business Requirements for use in the Capacity Plan. See Service Capacity Management. |
| Business Case | (Service Strategy) Justification for a significant item of expenditure. Includes information about Costs, benefits, options, issues, Risks, and possible problems. See Cost Benefit Analysis. |
| Business Continuity Management (BCM) | (Service Design) The Business Process responsible for managing Risks that could seriously impact the Business. BCM safeguards the interests of key stakeholders, reputation, brand and value creating activities. The BCM Process involves reducing Risks to an acceptable level and planning for the recovery of Business Processes should a disruption to the Business occur. BCM sets the Objectives, Scope and Requirements for IT Service Continuity Management. |
| Business Continuity Plan (BCP) | (Service Design) A Plan defining the steps required to Restore Business Processes following a disruption. The Plan will also identify the triggers for Invocation, people to be involved, communications etc. IT Service Continuity Plans form a significant part of Business Continuity Plans. |
| Business Customer | (Service Strategy) A recipient of a product or a Service from the Business. For example if the Business is a car manufacturer then the Business Customer is someone who buys a car. |

| | |
|---|---|
| Business Impact Analysis (BIA) | (Service Strategy) BIA is the Activity in Business Continuity Management that identifies Vital Business Functions and their dependencies. These dependencies may include Suppliers, people, other Business Processes, IT Services etc. BIA defines the recovery requirements for IT Services. These requirements include Recovery Time Objectives, Recovery Point Objectives and minimum Service Level Targets for each IT Service. |
| Business Objective | (Service Strategy) The Objective of a Business Process, or of the Business as a whole. Business Objectives support the Business Vision, provide guidance for the IT Strategy, and are often supported by IT Services. |
| Business Operations | (Service Strategy) The day-to-day execution, monitoring and management of Business Processes. |
| Business Perspective | (Continual Service Improvement) An understanding of the Service Provider and IT Services from the point of view of the Business, and an understanding of the Business from the point of view of the Service Provider. |
| Business Process | A Process that is owned and carried out by the Business. A Business Process contributes to the delivery of a product or Service to a Business Customer. For example, a retailer may have a purchasing Process which helps to deliver Services to their Business Customers. Many Business Processes rely on IT Services. |
| Business Relationship Management | (Service Strategy) The Process or Function responsible for maintaining a Relationship with the Business. BRM usually includes:<br>• Managing personal Relationships with Business managers<br>• Providing input to Service Portfolio Management<br>• Ensuring that the IT Service Provider is satisfying the Business needs of the Customers<br>This Process has strong links with Service Level Management. |
| Business Relationship Manager (BRM) | (Service Strategy) A Role responsible for maintaining the Relationship with one or more Customers. This Role is often combined with the Service Level Manager Role. See Account Manager. |
| Business Service | An IT Service that directly supports a Business Process, as opposed to an Infrastructure Service which is used internally by the IT Service Provider and is not usually visible to the Business. The term Business Service is also used to mean a Service that is delivered to Business Customers by Business Units. For example delivery of financial services to Customers of a bank, or goods to the Customers of a retail store. Successful delivery of Business Services often depends on one or more IT Services. |
| Business Service Management (BSM) | (Service Strategy) (Service Design) An approach to the management of IT Services that considers the Business Processes supported and the Business value provided. This term also means the management of Business Services delivered to Business Customers. |

| | |
|---|---|
| Business Unit | (Service Strategy) A segment of the Business which has its own Plans, Metrics, income and Costs. Each Business Unit owns Assets and uses these to create value for Customers in the form of goods and Services. |
| Call | (Service Operation) A telephone call to the Service Desk from a User. A Call could result in an Incident or a Service Request being logged. |
| Call Centre | (Service Operation) An Organization or Business Unit which handles large numbers of incoming and outgoing telephone calls. See Service Desk. |
| Call Type | (Service Operation) A Category that is used to distinguish incoming requests to a Service Desk. Common Call Types are Incident, Service Request and Complaint. |
| Capability | (Service Strategy) The ability of an Organization, person, Process, Application, Configuration Item or IT Service to carry out an Activity. Capabilities are intangible Assets of an Organization. See Resource. |
| Capability Maturity Model (CMM) | (Continual Service Improvement) The Capability Maturity Model for Software (also known as the CMM and SW-CMM) is a model used to identify Best Practices to help increase Process Maturity. CMM was developed at the Software Engineering Institute (SEI) of Carnegie Mellon University. In 2000, the SW-CMM was upgraded to CMMI® (Capability Maturity Model Integration). The SEI no longer maintains the SW-CMM model, its associated appraisal methods, or training materials. |
| Capability Maturity Model Integration (CMMI) | (Continual Service Improvement) Capability Maturity Model® Integration (CMMI) is a process improvement approach developed by the Software Engineering Institute (SEI) of Carnegie Melon University. CMMI provides organizations with the essential elements of effective processes. It can be used to guide process improvement across a project, a division, or an entire organization. CMMI helps integrate traditionally separate organizational functions, set process improvement goals and priorities, provide guidance for quality processes, and provide a point of reference for appraising current processes. See http://www.sei.cmu.edu/cmmi/ for more information. See CMM, Continuous Improvement, Maturity. |
| Capacity | (Service Design) The maximum Throughput that a Configuration Item or IT Service can deliver whilst meeting agreed Service Level Targets. For some types of CI, Capacity may be the size or volume, for example a disk drive. |
| Capacity Management | (Service Design) The Process responsible for ensuring that the Capacity of IT Services and the IT Infrastructure is able to deliver agreed Service Level Targets in a Cost Effective and timely manner. Capacity Management considers all Resources required to deliver the IT Service, and plans for short, medium and long term Business Requirements. |

| | |
|---|---|
| Capacity Management Information System (CMIS) | (Service Design) A virtual repository of all Capacity Management data, usually stored in multiple physical locations. See Service Knowledge Management System. |
| Capacity Plan | (Service Design) A Capacity Plan is used to manage the Resources required to deliver IT Services. The Plan contains scenarios for different predictions of Business demand, and costed options to deliver the agreed Service Level Targets. |
| Capacity Planning | (Service Design) The Activity within Capacity Management responsible for creating a Capacity Plan. |
| Capital Expenditure (CAPEX) | (Service Strategy) The Cost of purchasing something that will become a financial Asset, for example computer equipment and buildings. The value of the Asset is Depreciated over multiple accounting periods. |
| Capital Item | (Service Strategy) An Asset that is of interest to Financial Management because it is above an agreed financial value. |
| Capitalization | (Service Strategy) Identifying major Cost as capital, even though no Asset is purchased. This is done to spread the impact of the Cost over multiple accounting periods. The most common example of this is software development, or purchase of a software license. |
| Category | A named group of things that have something in common. Categories are used to group similar things together. For example Cost Types are used to group similar types of Cost. Incident Categories are used to group similar types of Incident, CI Types are used to group similar types of Configuration Item. |
| Certification | Issuing a certificate to confirm Compliance to a Standard. Certification includes a formal Audit by an independent and Accredited body. The term Certification is also used to mean awarding a certificate to verify that a person has achieved a qualification. |
| Change | (Service Transition) The addition, modification or removal of anything that could have an effect on IT Services. The Scope should include all IT Services, Configuration Items, Processes, Documentation etc. |
| Change Advisory Board (CAB) | (Service Transition) A group of people that advises the Change Manager in the Assessment, prioritization and scheduling of Changes. This board is usually made up of representatives from all areas within the IT Service Provider, the Business, and Third Parties such as Suppliers. |
| Change Case | (Service Operation) A technique used to predict the impact of proposed Changes. Change Cases use specific scenarios to clarify the scope of proposed Changes and to help with Cost Benefit Analysis. See Use Case. |

| | |
|---|---|
| Change History | (Service Transition) Information about all changes made to a Configuration Item during its life. Change History consists of all those Change Records that apply to the CI. |
| Change Management | (Service Transition) The Process responsible for controlling the Lifecycle of all Changes. The primary objective of Change Management is to enable beneficial Changes to be made, with minimum disruption to IT Services. |
| Change Model | (Service Transition) A repeatable way of dealing with a particular Category of Change. A Change Model defines specific pre-defined steps that will be followed for a Change of this Category. Change Models may be very simple, with no requirement for approval (e.g. Password Reset) or may be very complex with many steps that require approval (e.g. major software Release). See Standard Change, Change Advisory Board. |
| Change Record | (Service Transition) A Record containing the details of a Change. Each Change Record documents the Lifecycle of a single Change. A Change Record is created for every Request for Change that is received, even those that are subsequently rejected. Change Records should reference the Configuration Items that are affected by the Change. Change Records are stored in the Configuration Management System. |
| Change Request | Synonym for Request for Change. |
| Change Schedule | (Service Transition) A Document that lists all approved Changes and their planned implementation dates. A Change Schedule is sometimes called a Forward Schedule of Change, even though it also contains information about Changes that have already been implemented. |
| Change Window | (Service Transition) A regular, agreed time when Changes or Releases may be implemented with minimal impact on Services. Change Windows are usually documented in SLAs. |
| Charging | (Service Strategy) Requiring payment for IT Services. Charging for IT Services is optional, and many Organizations choose to treat their IT Service Provider as a Cost Centre. |
| Chronological Analysis | (Service Operation) A technique used to help identify possible causes of Problems. All available data about the Problem is collected and sorted by date and time to provide a detailed timeline. This can make it possible to identify which Events may have been triggered by others. |
| CI Type | (Service Transition) A Category that is used to Classify CIs. The CI Type identifies the required Attributes and Relationships for a Configuration Record. Common CI Types include: hardware, Document, User etc. |
| Classification | The act of assigning a Category to something. Classification is used to ensure consistent management and reporting. CIs, Incidents, Problems, Changes etc. are usually classified. |

| Client | A generic term that means a Customer, the Business or a Business Customer. For example Client Manager may be used as a synonym for Account Manager. The term client is also used to mean:<br>• A computer that is used directly by a User, for example a PC, Handheld Computer, or Workstation.<br>• The part of a Client-Server Application that the User directly interfaces with. For example an email Client. |
|---|---|
| Closed | (Service Operation) The final Status in the Lifecycle of an Incident, Problem, Change etc. When the Status is Closed, no further action is taken. |
| Closure | (Service Operation) The act of changing the Status of an Incident, Problem, Change etc. to Closed. |
| COBIT | (Continual Service Improvement) Control Objectives for Information and related Technology (COBIT) provides guidance and Best Practice for the management of IT Processes. COBIT is published by the IT Governance Institute. See http://www.isaca.org/ for more information. |
| Code of Practice | A Guideline published by a public body or a Standards Organization, such as ISO or BSI. Many Standards consist of a Code of Practice and a Specification. The Code of Practice describes recommended Best Practice. |
| Cold Standby | Synonym for Gradual Recovery. |
| Commercial off the Shelf (COTS) | (Service Design) Application software or Middleware that can be purchased from a Third Party. |
| Compliance | Ensuring that a Standard or set of Guidelines is followed, or that proper, consistent accounting or other practices are being employed. |
| Component | A general term that is used to mean one part of something more complex. For example, a computer System may be a component of an IT Service, an Application may be a Component of a Release Unit. Components that need to be managed should be Configuration Items. |
| Component Capacity Management (CCM) | (Service Design) (Continual Service Improvement) The Process responsible for understanding the Capacity, Utilization, and Performance of Configuration Items. Data is collected, recorded and analyzed for use in the Capacity Plan. See Service Capacity Management. |
| Component CI | (Service Transition) A Configuration Item that is part of an Assembly. For example, a CPU or Memory CI may be part of a Server CI. |
| Component Failure Impact Analysis (CFIA) | (Service Design) A technique that helps to identify the impact of CI failure on IT Services. A matrix is created with IT Services on one edge and CIs on the other. This enables the identification of critical CIs (that could cause the failure of multiple IT Services) and of fragile IT Services (that have multiple Single Points of Failure). |

| | |
|---|---|
| Computer Telephony Integration (CTI) | (Service Operation) CTI is a general term covering any kind of integration between computers and telephone Systems. It is most commonly used to refer to Systems where an Application displays detailed screens relating to incoming or outgoing telephone calls. See Automatic Call Distribution, Interactive Voice Response. |
| Concurrency | A measure of the number of Users engaged in the same Operation at the same time. |
| Confidentiality | (Service Design) A security principle that requires that data should only be accessed by authorized people. |
| Configuration | (Service Transition) A generic term, used to describe a group of Configuration Items that work together to deliver an IT Service, or a recognizable part of an IT Service. Configuration is also used to describe the parameter settings for one or more CIs. |
| Configuration Baseline | (Service Transition) A Baseline of a Configuration that has been formally agreed and is managed through the Change Management process. A Configuration Baseline is used as a basis for future Builds, Releases and Changes. |
| Configuration Control | (Service Transition) The Activity responsible for ensuring that adding, modifying or removing a CI is properly managed, for example by submitting a Request for Change or Service Request. |
| Configuration Identification | (Service Transition) The Activity responsible for collecting information about Configuration Items and their Relationships, and loading this information into the CMDB. Configuration Identification is also responsible for labeling the CIs themselves, so that the corresponding Configuration Records can be found. |
| Configuration Item (CI) | (Service Transition) Any Component that needs to be managed in order to deliver an IT Service. Information about each CI is recorded in a Configuration Record within the Configuration Management System and is maintained throughout its Lifecycle by Configuration Management. CIs are under the control of Change Management. CIs typically include IT Services, hardware, software, buildings, people, and formal documentation such as Process documentation and SLAs. |
| Configuration Management | (Service Transition) The Process responsible for maintaining information about Configuration Items required to deliver an IT Service, including their Relationships. This information is managed throughout the Lifecycle of the CI. Configuration Management is part of an overall Service Asset and Configuration Management Process. |
| Configuration Management Database (CMDB) | (Service Transition) A database used to store Configuration Records throughout their Lifecycle. The Configuration Management System maintains one or more CMDBs, and each CMDB stores Attributes of CIs, and Relationships with other CIs. |

| | |
|---|---|
| Configuration Management System (CMS) | (Service Transition) A set of tools and databases that are used to manage an IT Service Provider's Configuration data. The CMS also includes information about Incidents, Problems, Known Errors, Changes and Releases; and may contain data about employees, Suppliers, locations, Business Units, Customers and Users. The CMS includes tools for collecting, storing, managing, updating, and presenting data about all Configuration Items and their Relationships. The CMS is maintained by Configuration Management and is used by all IT Service Management Processes. See Configuration Management Database, Service Knowledge Management System. |
| Configuration Record | (Service Transition) A Record containing the details of a Configuration Item. Each Configuration Record documents the Lifecycle of a single CI. Configuration Records are stored in a Configuration Management Database. |
| Configuration Structure | (Service Transition) The hierarchy and other Relationships between all the Configuration Items that comprise a Configuration. |
| Continual Service Improvement (CSI) | (Continual Service Improvement) A stage in the Lifecycle of an IT Service and the title of one of the Core ITIL publications. Continual Service Improvement is responsible for managing improvements to IT Service Management Processes and IT Services. The Performance of the IT Service Provider is continually measured and improvements are made to Processes, IT Services and IT Infrastructure in order to increase Efficiency, Effectiveness, and Cost Effectiveness. See Plan-Do-Check-Act. |
| Continuous Availability | (Service Design) An approach or design to achieve 100% Availability. A Continuously Available IT Service has no planned or unplanned Downtime. |
| Continuous Operation | (Service Design) An approach or design to eliminate planned Downtime of an IT Service. Note that individual Configuration Items may be down even though the IT Service is Available. |
| Contract | A legally binding Agreement between two or more parties. |
| Contract Portfolio | (Service Strategy) A database or structured Document used to manage Service Contracts or Agreements between an IT Service Provider and their Customers. Each IT Service delivered to a Customer should have a Contract or other Agreement which is listed in the Contract Portfolio. See Service Portfolio, Service Catalogue. |
| Control | A means of managing a Risk, ensuring that a Business Objective is achieved, or ensuring that a Process is followed. Example Controls include Policies, Procedures, Roles, RAID, door-locks etc. A control is sometimes called a Countermeasure or safeguard. Control also means to manage the utilization or behavior of a Configuration Item, System or IT Service. |

| | |
|---|---|
| Control Objectives for Information and related Technology (COBIT) | See COBIT. |
| Control perspective | (Service Strategy) An approach to the management of IT Services, Processes, Functions, Assets etc. There can be several different Control Perspectives on the same IT Service, Process etc., allowing different individuals or teams to focus on what is important and relevant to their specific Role. Example Control Perspectives include Reactive and Proactive management within IT Operations, or a Lifecycle view for an Application Project team. |
| Control Processes | The ISO/IEC 20000 Process group that includes Change Management and Configuration Management. |
| Core Service | (Service Strategy) An IT Service that delivers basic Outcomes desired by one or more Customers. See Supporting Service, Core Service Package. |
| Core Service Package (CSP) | (Service Strategy) A detailed description of a Core Service that may be shared by two or more Service Level Packages. See Service Package. |
| Cost | The amount of money spent on a specific Activity, IT Service, or Business Unit. Costs consist of real cost (money), notional cost such as people's time, and Depreciation. |
| Cost Benefit Analysis | An Activity that analyses and compares the Costs and the benefits involved in one or more alternative courses of action. See Business Case, Net Present Value, Internal Rate of Return, Return on Investment, Value on Investment. |
| Cost Centre | (Service Strategy) A Business Unit or Project to which Costs are assigned. A Cost Centre does not charge for Services provided. An IT Service Provider can be run as a Cost Centre or a Profit Centre. |
| Cost Effectiveness | A measure of the balance between the Effectiveness and Cost of a Service, Process or activity, A Cost Effective Process is one which achieves its Objectives at minimum Cost. See KPI, Return on Investment, Value for Money. |
| Cost Element | (Service Strategy) The middle level of category to which Costs are assigned in Budgeting and Accounting. The highest level category is Cost Type. For example a Cost Type of "people" could have cost elements of payroll, staff benefits, expenses, training, overtime etc. Cost Elements can be further broken down to give Cost Units. For example the Cost Element "expenses" could include Cost Units of Hotels, Transport, Meals etc. |
| Cost Management | (Service Strategy) A general term that is used to refer to Budgeting and Accounting, sometimes used as a synonym for Financial Management |

Cost Type            (Service Strategy) The highest level of category to which Costs are assigned
                     in Budgeting and Accounting. For example hardware, software, people,
                     accommodation, external and Transfer.
                     See Cost Element, Cost Type.

Cost Unit            (Service Strategy) The lowest level of category to which Costs are assigned, Cost
                     Units are usually things that can be easily counted (e.g. staff numbers, software
                     licenses) or things easily measured (e.g. CPU usage, Electricity consumed).
                     Cost Units are included within Cost Elements. For example a Cost Element of
                     "expenses" could include Cost Units of Hotels, Transport, Meals etc.
                     See Cost Type.

Countermeasure       Can be used to refer to any type of Control. The term Countermeasure is most
                     often used when referring to measures that increase Resilience, Fault Tolerance or
                     Reliability of an IT Service.

Course Corrections   Changes made to a Plan or Activity that has already started, to ensure that it
                     will meet its Objectives. Course corrections are made as a result of Monitoring
                     progress.

CRAMM                A methodology and tool for analyzing and managing Risks. CRAMM was
                     developed by the UK Government, but is now privately owned.
                     Further information is available from http://www.cramm.com/

Crisis Management    The Process responsible for managing the wider implications of Business
                     Continuity. A Crisis Management team is responsible for Strategic issues such as
                     managing media relations and shareholder confidence, and decides when to invoke
                     Business Continuity Plans.

Critical Success     Something that must happen if a Process, Project, Plan, or IT Service is to succeed.
Factor (CSF)         KPIs are used to measure the achievement of each CSF. For example a CSF of
                     "protect IT Services when making Changes" could be measured by KPIs such
                     as "percentage reduction of unsuccessful Changes", "percentage reduction in
                     Changes causing Incidents" etc.

Culture              A set of values that is shared by a group of people, including expectations about
                     how people should behave, ideas, beliefs, and practices.
                     See Vision.

Customer             Someone who buys goods or Services. The Customer of an IT Service Provider is
                     the person or group who defines and agrees the Service Level Targets. The term
                     Customers is also sometimes informally used to mean Users, for example "this is a
                     Customer focused Organization".

Customer Portfolio   (Service Strategy) A database or structured Document used to record all
                     Customers of the IT Service Provider. The Customer Portfolio is the Business
                     Relationship Manager's view of the Customers who receive Services from the IT
                     Service Provider.
                     See Contract Portfolio, Service Portfolio.

| | |
|---|---|
| Dashboard | (Service Operation) A graphical representation of overall IT Service Performance and Availability. Dashboard images may be updated in real-time, and can also be included in management reports and web pages. Dashboards can be used to support Service Level Management, Event Management or Incident Diagnosis. |
| Data-to-Information-to-Knowledge-to-Wisdom (DIKW) | A way of understanding the relationships between data, information, knowledge, and wisdom. DIKW shows how each of these builds on the others. |
| Definitive Media Library (DML) | (Service Transition) One or more locations in which the definitive and approved versions of all software Configuration Items are securely stored. The DML may also contain associated CIs such as licenses and documentation. The DML is a single logical storage area even if there are multiple locations. All software in the DML is under the control of Change and Release Management and is recorded in the Configuration Management System. Only software from the DML is acceptable for use in a Release. |
| Deliverable | Something that must be provided to meet a commitment in a Service Level Agreement or a Contract. Deliverable is also used in a more informal way to mean a planned output of any Process. |
| Demand Management | Activities that understand and influence Customer demand for Services and the provision of Capacity to meet these demands. At a Strategic level Demand Management can involve analysis of Patterns of Business Activity and User Profiles. At a Tactical level it can involve use of Differential Charging to encourage Customers to use IT Services at less busy times. See Capacity Management. |
| Deming Cycle | Synonym for Plan Do Check Act. |
| Dependency | The direct or indirect reliance of one Process or Activity upon another. |
| Deployment | (Service Transition) The Activity responsible for movement of new or changed hardware, software, documentation, Process, etc to the Live Environment. Deployment is part of the Release and Deployment Management Process. See Rollout. |
| Depreciation | (Service Strategy) A measure of the reduction in value of an Asset over its life. This is based on wearing out, consumption or other reduction in the useful economic value. |
| Design | (Service Design) An Activity or Process that identifies Requirements and then defines a solution that is able to meet these Requirements. See Service Design. |
| Detection | (Service Operation) A stage in the Incident Lifecycle. Detection results in the Incident becoming known to the Service Provider. Detection can be automatic, or can be the result of a User logging an Incident. |

| | |
|---|---|
| Development | (Service Design) The Process responsible for creating or modifying an IT Service or Application. Also used to mean the Role or group that carries out Development work. |
| Development Environment | (Service Design) An Environment used to create or modify IT Services or Applications. Development Environments are not typically subjected to the same degree of control as Test Environments or Live Environments.<br>See Development. |
| Diagnosis | (Service Operation) A stage in the Incident and Problem Lifecycles. The purpose of Diagnosis is to identify a Workaround for an Incident or the Root Cause of a Problem. |
| Diagnostic Script | (Service Operation) A structured set of questions used by Service Desk staff to ensure they ask the correct questions, and to help them Classify, Resolve and assign Incidents. Diagnostic Scripts may also be made available to Users to help them diagnose and resolve their own Incidents. |
| Differential Charging | A technique used to support Demand Management by charging different amounts for the same IT Service Function at different times. |
| Direct Cost | (Service Strategy) A cost of providing an IT Service which can be allocated in full to a specific Customer, Cost Centre, Project etc. For example cost of providing non-shared servers or software licenses.<br>See Indirect Cost. |
| Directory Service | (Service Operation) An Application that manages information about IT Infrastructure available on a network, and corresponding User access Rights. |
| Do Nothing | (Service Design) A Recovery Option. The Service Provider formally agrees with the Customer that Recovery of this IT Service will not be performed. |
| Document | Information in readable form. A Document may be paper or electronic. For example a Policy statement, Service Level Agreement, Incident Record, diagram of computer room layout.<br>See Record. |
| Downtime | (Service Design) (Service Operation) The time when a Configuration Item or IT Service is not Available during its Agreed Service Time. The Availability of an IT Service is often calculated from Agreed Service Time and Downtime. |
| Driver | Something that influences Strategy, Objectives or Requirements. For example new legislation or the actions of competitors. |
| Early Life Support | (Service Transition) Support provided for a new or Changed IT Service for a period of time after it is Released. During Early Life Support the IT Service Provider may review the KPIs, Service Levels and Monitoring Thresholds, and provide additional Resources for Incident and Problem Management. |

| | |
|---|---|
| Economies of scale | (Service Strategy) The reduction in average Cost that is possible from increasing the usage of an IT Service or Asset.<br>See Economies of Scope. |
| Economies of scope | (Service Strategy) The reduction in Cost that is allocated to an IT Service by using an existing Asset for an additional purpose. For example delivering a new IT Service from existing IT Infrastructure.<br>See Economies of Scale. |
| Effectiveness | (Continual Service Improvement) A measure of whether the Objectives of a Process, Service or Activity have been achieved. An Effective Process or Activity is one that achieves its agreed Objectives.<br>See KPI. |
| Efficiency | (Continual Service Improvement) A measure of whether the right amount of resources have been used to deliver a Process, Service or Activity. An Efficient Process achieves its Objectives with the minimum amount of time, money, people or other resources.<br>See KPI. |
| Emergency Change | (Service Transition) A Change that must be introduced as soon as possible. For example to resolve a Major Incident or implement a Security patch. The Change Management Process will normally have a specific Procedure for handling Emergency Changes.<br>See Emergency Change Advisory Board (ECAB). |
| Emergency Change Advisory Board (ECAB) | (Service Transition) A sub-set of the Change Advisory Board who make decisions about high impact Emergency Changes. Membership of the ECAB may be decided at the time a meeting is called, and depends on the nature of the Emergency Change. |
| Environment | (Service Transition) A subset of the IT Infrastructure that is used for a particular purpose. For Example: Live Environment, Test Environment, Build Environment. It is possible for multiple Environments to share a Configuration Item, for example Test and Live Environments may use different partitions on a single mainframe computer. Also used in the term Physical Environment to mean the accommodation, air conditioning, power system etc.<br>Environment is also used as a generic term to mean the external conditions that influence or affect something. |
| Error | (Service Operation) A design flaw or malfunction that causes a Failure of one or more Configuration Items or IT Services. A mistake made by a person or a faulty Process that impacts a CI or IT Service is also an Error. |

| Escalation | (Service Operation) An Activity that obtains additional Resources when these are needed to meet Service Level Targets or Customer expectations. Escalation may be needed within any IT Service Management Process, but is most commonly associated with Incident Management, Problem Management and the management of Customer complaints. There are two types of Escalation, Functional Escalation and Hierarchic Escalation. |
|---|---|
| eSourcing Capability Model for Client Organizations (eSCM-CL) | (Service Strategy) A framework to help Organizations guide their analysis and decisions on Service Sourcing Models and Strategies. eSCM-CL was developed by Carnegie Mellon University. See eSCM-SP. |
| eSourcing Capability Model for Service Providers (eSCM-SP) | (Service Strategy) A framework to help IT Service Providers develop their IT Service Management Capabilities from a Service Sourcing perspective. eSCM-SP was developed by Carnegie Mellon University. See eSCM-CL. |
| Estimation | The use of experience to provide an approximate value for a Metric or Cost. Estimation is also used in Capacity and Availability Management as the cheapest and least accurate Modeling method. |
| Evaluation | (Service Transition) The Process responsible for assessing a new or Changed IT Service to ensure that Risks have been managed and to help determine whether to proceed with the Change. Evaluation is also used to mean comparing an actual Outcome with the intended Outcome, or comparing one alternative with another. |
| Event | (Service Operation) A change of state which has significance for the management of a Configuration Item or IT Service. The term Event is also used to mean an Alert or notification created by any IT Service, Configuration Item or Monitoring tool. Events typically require IT Operations personnel to take actions, and often lead to Incidents being logged. |
| Event Management | (Service Operation) The Process responsible for managing Events throughout their Lifecycle. Event Management is one of the main Activities of IT Operations. |
| Exception Report | A Document containing details of one or more KPIs or other important targets that have exceeded defined Thresholds. Examples include SLA targets being missed or about to be missed, and a Performance Metric indicating a potential Capacity problem. |
| Expanded Incident Lifecycle | (Availability Management) Detailed stages in the Lifecycle of an Incident. The stages are Detection, Diagnosis, Repair, Recovery, Restoration. The Expanded Incident Lifecycle is used to help understand all contributions to the Impact of Incidents and to Plan how these could be controlled or reduced. |
| External Customer | A Customer who works for a different Business to the IT Service Provider. See External Service Provider, Internal Customer. |

| | |
|---|---|
| External Metric | A Metric that is used to measure the delivery of IT Service to a Customer. External Metrics are usually defined in SLAs and reported to Customers. See Internal Metric. |
| External Service Provider | (Service Strategy) An IT Service Provider which is part of a different Organization to their Customer. An IT Service Provider may have both Internal Customers and External Customers. See Type III Service Provider. |
| External Sourcing | Synonym for Outsourcing. |
| Facilities Management | (Service Operation) The Function responsible for managing the physical Environment where the IT Infrastructure is located. Facilities Management includes all aspects of managing the physical Environment, for example power and cooling, building Access Management, and environmental Monitoring. |
| Failure | (Service Operation) Loss of ability to Operate to Specification, or to deliver the required output. The term Failure may be used when referring to IT Services, Processes, Activities, Configuration Items etc. A Failure often causes an Incident. |
| Failure Modes and Effects Analysis (FMEA) | An approach to assessing the potential Impact of Failures. FMEA involves analyzing what would happen after Failure of each Configuration Item, all the way up to the effect on the Business. FMEA is often used in Information Security Management and in IT Service Continuity Planning. |
| Fast Recovery | (Service Design) A Recovery Option which is also known as Hot Standby. Provision is made to Recover the IT Service in a short period of time, typically less than 24 hours. Fast Recovery typically uses a dedicated Fixed Facility with computer Systems, and software configured ready to run the IT Services. Immediate Recovery may take up to 24 hours if there is a need to Restore data from Backups. |
| Fault | Synonym for Error. |
| Fault Tolerance | (Service Design) The ability of an IT Service or Configuration Item to continue to Operate correctly after Failure of a Component part. See Resilience, Countermeasure. |
| Fault Tree Analysis (FTA) | (Service Design) (Continual Service Improvement) A technique that can be used to determine the chain of Events that leads to a Problem. Fault Tree Analysis represents a chain of Events using Boolean notation in a diagram. |
| Financial Management | (Service Strategy) The Function and Processes responsible for managing an IT Service Provider's Budgeting, Accounting and Charging Requirements. |
| First-line Support | (Service Operation) The first level in a hierarchy of Support Groups involved in the resolution of Incidents. Each level contains more specialist skills, or has more time or other Resources. See Escalation. |
| Fishbone Diagram | Synonym for Ishikawa Diagram. |

| | |
|---|---|
| Fit for Purpose | An informal term used to describe a Process, Configuration Item, IT Service etc. that is capable of meeting its Objectives or Service Levels. Being Fit for Purpose requires suitable Design, implementation, Control and maintenance. |
| Fixed Cost | (Service Strategy) A Cost that does not vary with IT Service usage. For example the cost of Server hardware.<br>See Variable Cost. |
| Fixed Facility | (Service Design) A permanent building, available for use when needed by an IT Service Continuity Plan.<br>See Recovery Option, Portable Facility. |
| Follow the Sun | (Service Operation) A methodology for using Service Desks and Support Groups around the world to provide seamless 24 * 7 Service. Calls, Incidents, Problems and Service Requests are passed between groups in different time zones. |
| Fulfilment | Performing Activities to meet a need or Requirement. For example by providing a new IT Service, or meeting a Service Request. |
| Function | A team or group of people and the tools they use to carry out one or more Processes or Activities. For example the Service Desk.<br>The term Function also has two other meanings<br>•   An intended purpose of a Configuration Item, Person, Team, Process, or IT Service. For example one Function of an Email Service may be to store and forward outgoing mails, one Function of a Business Process may be to dispatch goods to Customers.<br>•   To perform the intended purpose correctly, "The computer is Functioning" |
| Functional Escalation | (Service Operation) Transferring an Incident, Problem or Change to a technical team with a higher level of expertise to assist in an Escalation. |
| Gap Analysis | (Continual Service Improvement) An Activity which compares two sets of data and identifies the differences. Gap Analysis is commonly used to compare a set of Requirements with actual delivery.<br>See Benchmarking. |
| Governance | Ensuring that Policies and Strategy are actually implemented, and that required Processes are correctly followed. Governance includes defining Roles and responsibilities, measuring and reporting, and taking actions to resolve any issues identified. |
| Gradual Recovery | (Service Design) A Recovery Option which is also known as Cold Standby. Provision is made to Recover the IT Service in a period of time greater than 72 hours. Gradual Recovery typically uses a Portable or Fixed Facility that has environmental support and network cabling, but no computer Systems. The hardware and software are installed as part of the IT Service Continuity Plan. |
| Guideline | A Document describing Best Practice, that recommends what should be done. Compliance to a guideline is not normally enforced.<br>See Standard. |

| Help Desk | (Service Operation) A point of contact for Users to log Incidents. A Help Desk is usually more technically focused than a Service Desk and does not provide a Single Point of Contact for all interaction. The term Help Desk is often used as a synonym for Service Desk. |
|---|---|
| Hierarchic Escalation | (Service Operation) Informing or involving more senior levels of management to assist in an Escalation. |
| High Availability | (Service Design) An approach or Design that minimizes or hides the effects of Configuration Item Failure on the Users of an IT Service. High Availability solutions are Designed to achieve an agreed level of Availability and make use of techniques such as Fault Tolerance, Resilience and fast Recovery to reduce the number of Incidents, and the Impact of Incidents. |
| Hot Standby | Synonym for Fast Recovery or Immediate Recovery. |
| Identity | (Service Operation) A unique name that is used to identify a User, person or Role. The Identity is used to grant Rights to that User, person, or Role. Example identities might be the username SmithJ or the Role "Change manager". |
| Immediate Recovery | (Service Design) A Recovery Option which is also known as Hot Standby. Provision is made to Recover the IT Service with no loss of Service. Immediate Recovery typically uses mirroring, load balancing and split site technologies. |
| Impact | (Service Operation) (Service Transition) A measure of the effect of an Incident, Problem or Change on Business Processes. Impact is often based on how Service Levels will be affected. Impact and Urgency are used to assign Priority. |
| Incident | (Service Operation) An unplanned interruption to an IT Service or a reduction in the Quality of an IT Service. Failure of a Configuration Item that has not yet impacted Service is also an Incident. For example Failure of one disk from a mirror set. |
| Incident Management | (Service Operation) The Process responsible for managing the Lifecycle of all Incidents. The primary Objective of Incident Management is to return the IT Service to Users as quickly as possible. |
| Incident Record | (Service Operation) A Record containing the details of an Incident. Each Incident record documents the Lifecycle of a single Incident. |
| Indirect Cost | (Service Strategy) A Cost of providing an IT Service which cannot be allocated in full to a specific Customer. For example Cost of providing shared Servers or software licenses. Also known as Overhead. See Direct Cost. |

| | |
|---|---|
| Information Security Management (ISM) | (Service Design) The Process that ensures the Confidentiality, Integrity and Availability of an Organization's Assets, information, data and IT Services. Information Security Management usually forms part of an Organizational approach to Security Management which has a wider scope than the IT Service Provider, and includes handling of paper, building access, phone calls etc., for the entire Organization. |
| Information Security Management System (ISMS) | (Service Design) The framework of Policy, Processes, Standards, Guidelines and tools that ensures an Organization can achieve its Information Security Management Objectives. |
| Information Security Policy | (Service Design) The Policy that governs the Organization's approach to Information Security Management. |
| Information Technology (IT) | The use of technology for the storage, communication or processing of information. The technology typically includes computers, telecommunications, Applications and other software. The information may include Business data, voice, images, video, etc. Information Technology is often used to support Business Processes through IT Services. |
| Infrastructure Service | An IT Service that is not directly used by the Business, but is required by the IT Service Provider so they can provide other IT Services. For example Directory Services, naming services, or communication services. |
| Insourcing | Synonym for Internal Sourcing. |
| Integrity | (Service Design) A security principle that ensures data and Configuration Items are only modified by authorized personnel and Activities. Integrity considers all possible causes of modification, including software and hardware Failure, environmental Events, and human intervention. |
| Interactive Voice Response (IVR) | (Service Operation) A form of Automatic Call Distribution that accepts User input, such as key presses and spoken commands, to identify the correct destination for incoming Calls. |
| Intermediate Recovery | (Service Design) A Recovery Option which is also known as Warm Standby. Provision is made to Recover the IT Service in a period of time between 24 and 72 hours. Intermediate Recovery typically uses a shared Portable or Fixed Facility that has computer Systems and network Components. The hardware and software will need to be configured, and data will need to be restored, as part of the IT Service Continuity Plan. |
| Internal Customer | A Customer who works for the same Business as the IT Service Provider. See Internal Service Provider, External Customer. |
| Internal Metric | A Metric that is used within the IT Service Provider to Monitor the Efficiency, Effectiveness or Cost Effectiveness of the IT Service Provider's internal Processes. Internal Metrics are not normally reported to the Customer of the IT Service. See External Metric. |

| | |
|---|---|
| Internal Rate of Return (IRR) | (Service Strategy) A technique used to help make decisions about Capital Expenditure. IRR calculates a figure that allows two or more alternative investments to be compared. A larger IRR indicates a better investment. See Net Present Value, Return on Investment. |
| Internal Service Provider | (Service Strategy) An IT Service Provider which is part of the same Organization as their Customer. An IT Service Provider may have both Internal Customers and External Customers. See Type I Service Provider, Type II Service Provider, Insource. |
| Internal Sourcing | (Service Strategy) Using an Internal Service Provider to manage IT Services. See Service Sourcing, Type I Service Provider, Type II Service Provider. |
| International Organization for Standardization (ISO) | The International Organization for Standardization (ISO) is the world's largest developer of Standards. ISO is a non-governmental organization which is a network of the national standards institutes of 156 countries. Further information about ISO is available from http://www.iso.org/ |
| International Standards Organization | See International Organization for Standardization (ISO) |
| Internet Service Provider (ISP) | An External Service Provider that provides access to the Internet. Most ISPs also provide other IT Services such as web hosting. |
| Invocation | (Service Design) Initiation of the steps defined in a plan. For example initiating the IT Service Continuity Plan for one or more IT Services. |
| Ishikawa Diagram | (Service Operation) (Continual Service Improvement) A technique that helps a team to identify all the possible causes of a Problem. Originally devised by Kaoru Ishikawa, the output of this technique is a diagram that looks like a fishbone. |
| ISO 9000 | A generic term that refers to a number of international Standards and Guidelines for Quality Management Systems. See http://www.iso.org/ for more information. See ISO. |
| ISO 9001 | An international Standard for Quality Management Systems. See ISO 9000, Standard. |
| ISO/IEC 17799 | (Continual Service Improvement) ISO Code of Practice for Information Security Management. See Standard. |
| ISO/IEC 20000 | ISO Specification and Code of Practice for IT Service Management. ISO/IEC 20000 is aligned with ITIL Best Practice. |

| | |
|---|---|
| ISO/IEC 27001 | (Service Design) (Continual Service Improvement) ISO Specification for Information Security Management. The corresponding Code of Practice is ISO/IEC 17799.<br>See Standard. |
| IT Directorate | (Continual Service Improvement) Senior Management within a Service Provider, charged with developing and delivering IT services. Most commonly used in UK Government departments. |
| IT Infrastructure | All of the hardware, software, networks, facilities etc. that are required to Develop, Test, deliver, Monitor, Control or support IT Services. The term IT Infrastructure includes all of the Information Technology but not the associated people, Processes and documentation. |
| IT Operations | (Service Operation) Activities carried out by IT Operations Control, including Console Management, Job Scheduling, Backup and Restore, and Print and Output Management.<br>IT Operations is also used as a synonym for Service Operation. |
| IT Operations Control | (Service Operation) The Function responsible for Monitoring and Control of the IT Services and IT Infrastructure.<br>See Operations Bridge. |
| IT Operations Management | (Service Operation) The Function within an IT Service Provider which performs the daily Activities needed to manage IT Services and the supporting IT Infrastructure. IT Operations Management includes IT Operations Control and Facilities Management. |
| IT Service | A Service provided to one or more Customers by an IT Service Provider. An IT Service is based on the use of Information Technology and supports the Customer's Business Processes. An IT Service is made up from a combination of people, Processes and technology and should be defined in a Service Level Agreement. |
| IT Service Continuity Management (ITSCM) | (Service Design) The Process responsible for managing Risks that could seriously impact IT Services. ITSCM ensures that the IT Service Provider can always provide minimum agreed Service Levels, by reducing the Risk to an acceptable level and Planning for the Recovery of IT Services. ITSCM should be designed to support Business Continuity Management. |
| IT Service Continuity Plan | (Service Design) A Plan defining the steps required to Recover one or more IT Services. The Plan will also identify the triggers for Invocation, people to be involved, communications etc. The IT Service Continuity Plan should be part of a Business Continuity Plan. |
| IT Service Management (ITSM) | The implementation and management of Quality IT Services that meet the needs of the Business. IT Service Management is performed by IT Service Providers through an appropriate mix of people, Process and Information Technology.<br>See Service Management. |

| | |
|---|---|
| IT Service Management Forum (itSMF) | The IT Service Management Forum is an independent Organization dedicated to promoting a professional approach to IT Service Management. The itSMF is a not-for-profit membership Organization with representation in many countries around the world (itSMF Chapters). The itSMF and its membership contribute to the development of ITIL and associated IT Service Management Standards. See http://www.itsmf.com/ for more information. |
| IT Service Provider | (Service Strategy) A Service Provider that provides IT Services to Internal Customers or External Customers. |
| IT Steering Group (ISG) | A formal group that is responsible for ensuring that Business and IT Service Provider Strategies and Plans are closely aligned. An IT Steering Group includes senior representatives from the Business and the IT Service Provider. |
| ITIL | A set of Best Practice guidance for IT Service Management. ITIL is owned by the OGC and consists of a series of publications giving guidance on the provision of Quality IT Services, and on the Processes and facilities needed to support them. See http://www.itil.co.uk/ for more information. |
| Job Description | A Document which defines the Roles, responsibilities, skills and knowledge required by a particular person. One Job Description can include multiple Roles, for example the Roles of Configuration Manager and Change Manager may be carried out by one person. |
| Job Scheduling | (Service Operation) Planning and managing the execution of software tasks that are required as part of an IT Service. Job Scheduling is carried out by IT Operations Management, and is often automated using software tools that run batch or online tasks at specific times of the day, week, month or year. |
| Kano Model | (Service Strategy) A Model developed by Noriaki Kano that is used to help understand Customer preferences. The Kano Model considers Attributes of an IT Service grouped into areas such as Basic Factors, Excitement Factors, Performance Factors etc. |
| Kepner & Tregoe Analysis | (Service Operation) (Continual Service Improvement) A structured approach to Problem solving. The Problem is analyzed in terms of what, where, when and extent. Possible causes are identified. The most probable cause is tested. The true cause is verified. |
| Key Performance Indicator (KPI) | (Continual Service Improvement) A Metric that is used to help manage a Process, IT Service or Activity. Many Metrics may be measured, but only the most important of these are defined as KPIs and used to actively manage and report on the Process, IT Service or Activity. KPIs should be selected to ensure that Efficiency, Effectiveness, and Cost Effectiveness are all managed. See Critical Success Factor. |
| Knowledge Base | (Service Transition) A logical database containing the data used by the Service Knowledge Management System. |

| Knowledge Management | (Service Transition) The Process responsible for gathering, analyzing, storing and sharing knowledge and information within an Organization. The primary purpose of Knowledge Management is to improve Efficiency by reducing the need to rediscover knowledge.<br>See Data-to-Information-to-Knowledge-to-Wisdom, Service Knowledge Management System. |
|---|---|
| Known Error | (Service Operation) A Problem that has a documented Root Cause and a Workaround. Known Errors are created and managed throughout their Lifecycle by Problem Management. Known Errors may also be identified by Development or Suppliers. |
| Known Error Database (KEDB) | (Service Operation) A database containing all Known Error Records. This database is created by Problem Management and used by Incident and Problem Management. The Known Error Database is part of the Service Knowledge Management System. |
| Known Error Record | (Service Operation) A Record containing the details of a Known Error. Each Known Error Record documents the Lifecycle of a Known Error, including the Status, Root Cause and Workaround. In some implementations a Known Error is documented using additional fields in a Problem Record. |
| Lifecycle | The various stages in the life of an IT Service, Configuration Item, Incident, Problem, Change etc. The Lifecycle defines the Categories for Status and the Status transitions that are permitted. For example:<br>• The Lifecycle of an Application includes Requirements, Design, Build, Deploy, Operate, Optimize.<br>• The Expanded Incident Lifecycle includes Detect, Respond, Diagnose, Repair, Recover, Restore.<br>• The lifecycle of a Server may include: Ordered, Received, In Test, Live, Disposed etc. |
| Line of Service (LOS) | (Service Strategy) A Core Service or Supporting Service that has multiple Service Level Packages. A line of Service is managed by a Product Manager and each Service Level Package is designed to support a particular market segment. |
| Live | (Service Transition) Refers to an IT Service or Configuration Item that is being used to deliver Service to a Customer. |
| Live Environment | (Service Transition) A controlled Environment containing Live Configuration Items used to deliver IT Services to Customers. |
| Maintainability | (Service Design) A measure of how quickly and Effectively a Configuration Item or IT Service can be restored to normal working after a Failure. Maintainability is often measured and reported as MTRS.<br>Maintainability is also used in the context of Software or IT Service Development to mean ability to be Changed or Repaired easily. |

| | |
|---|---|
| Major Incident | (Service Operation) The highest Category of Impact for an Incident. A Major Incident results in significant disruption to the Business. |
| Managed Services | (Service Strategy) A perspective on IT Services which emphasizes the fact that they are managed. The term Managed Services is also used as a synonym for Outsourced IT Services. |
| Management Information | Information that is used to support decision making by managers. Management Information is often generated automatically by tools supporting the various IT Service Management Processes. Management Information often includes the values of KPIs such as "Percentage of Changes leading to Incidents", or "first time fix rate". |
| Management of Risk (MoR) | The OGC methodology for managing Risks. MoR includes all the Activities required to identify and Control the exposure to Risk which may have an impact on the achievement of an Organization's Business Objectives. See http://www.m-o-r.org/ for more details. |
| Management System | The framework of Policy, Processes and Functions that ensures an Organization can achieve its Objectives. |
| Manual Workaround | A Workaround that requires manual intervention. Manual Workaround is also used as the name of a Recovery Option in which The Business Process Operates without the use of IT Services. This is a temporary measure and is usually combined with another Recovery Option. |
| Marginal Cost | (Service Strategy) The Cost of continuing to provide the IT Service. Marginal Cost does not include investment already made, for example the cost of developing new software and delivering training. |
| Market Space | (Service Strategy) All opportunities that an IT Service Provider could exploit to meet business needs of Customers. The Market Space identifies the possible IT Services that an IT Service Provider may wish to consider delivering. |
| Maturity | (Continual Service Improvement) A measure of the Reliability, Efficiency and Effectiveness of a Process, Function, Organization etc. The most mature Processes and Functions are formally aligned to Business Objectives and Strategy, and are supported by a framework for continual improvement. |
| Maturity Level | A named level in a Maturity model such as the Carnegie Mellon Capability Maturity Model Integration. |
| Mean Time Between Failures (MTBF) | (Service Design) A Metric for measuring and reporting Reliability. MTBF is the average time that a Configuration Item or IT Service can perform its agreed Function without interruption. This is measured from when the CI or IT Service starts working, until it next fails. |
| Mean Time Between Service Incidents (MTBSI) | (Service Design) A Metric used for measuring and reporting Reliability. MTBSI is the mean time from when a System or IT Service fails, until it next fails. MTBSI is equal to MTBF + MTRS. |

| | |
|---|---|
| Mean Time To Repair (MTTR) | The average time taken to repair a Configuration Item or IT Service after a Failure. MTTR is measured from when the CI or IT Service fails until it is Repaired. MTTR does not include the time required to Recover or Restore. MTTR is sometimes incorrectly used to mean Mean Time to Restore Service. |
| Mean Time to Restore Service (MTRS) | The average time taken to Restore a Configuration Item or IT Service after a Failure. MTRS is measured from when the CI or IT Service fails until it is fully Restored and delivering its normal functionality. See Maintainability, Mean Time to Repair. |
| Metric | (Continual Service Improvement) Something that is measured and reported to help manage a Process, IT Service or Activity. See KPI. |
| Middleware | (Service Design) Software that connects two or more software Components or Applications. Middleware is usually purchased from a Supplier, rather than developed within the IT Service Provider. See Off the Shelf. |
| Mission Statement | The Mission Statement of an Organization is a short but complete description of the overall purpose and intentions of that Organization. It states what is to be achieved, but not how this should be done. |
| Model | A representation of a System, Process, IT Service, Configuration Item etc. that is used to help understand or predict future behavior. |
| Modeling | A technique that is used to predict the future behavior of a System, Process, IT Service, Configuration Item etc. Modeling is commonly used in Financial Management, Capacity Management and Availability Management. |
| Monitor Control Loop | (Service Operation) Monitoring the output of a Task, Process, IT Service or Configuration Item; comparing this output to a predefined norm; and taking appropriate action based on this comparison. |
| Monitoring | (Service Operation) Repeated observation of a Configuration Item, IT Service or Process to detect Events and to ensure that the current status is known. |
| Near-Shore | (Service Strategy) Provision of Services from a country near the country where the Customer is based. This can be the provision of an IT Service, or of supporting Functions such as Service Desk. See On-shore, Off-shore. |
| Net Present Value (NPV) | (Service Strategy) A technique used to help make decisions about Capital Expenditure. NPV compares cash inflows to cash outflows. Positive NPV indicates that an investment is worthwhile. See Internal Rate of Return, Return on Investment. |

| | |
|---|---|
| Notional Charging | (Service Strategy) An approach to Charging for IT Services. Charges to Customers are calculated and Customers are informed of the charge, but no money is actually transferred. Notional Charging is sometimes introduced to ensure that Customers are aware of the Costs they incur, or as a stage during the introduction of real Charging. |
| Objective | The defined purpose or aim of a Process, an Activity or an Organization as a whole. Objectives are usually expressed as measurable targets. The term Objective is also informally used to mean a Requirement. See Outcome. |
| Off the Shelf | Synonym for Commercial Off the Shelf. |
| Office of Government Commerce (OGC) | OGC owns the ITIL brand (copyright and trademark). OGC is a UK Government department that supports the delivery of the government's procurement agenda through its work in collaborative procurement and in raising levels of procurement skills and capability with departments. It also provides support for complex public sector projects. |
| Office of Public Sector Information (OPSI) | OPSI license the Crown Copyright material used in the ITIL publications. They are a UK Government department who provide online access to UK legislation, license the re-use of Crown copyright material, manage the Information Fair Trader Scheme, maintain the Government's Information Asset Register and provide advice and guidance on official publishing and Crown copyright. |
| Off-shore | (Service Strategy) Provision of Services from a location outside the country where the Customer is based, often in a different continent. This can be the provision of an IT Service, or of supporting Functions such as Service Desk. See On-shore, Near-shore. |
| On-shore | (Service Strategy) Provision of Services from a location within the country where the Customer is based. See Off-shore, Near-shore. |
| Operate | To perform as expected. A Process or Configuration Item is said to Operate if it is delivering the Required outputs. Operate also means to perform one or more Operations. For example, to Operate a computer is to do the day-to-day Operations needed for it to perform as expected. |
| Operation | (Service Operation) Day-to-day management of an IT Service, System, or other Configuration Item. Operation is also used to mean any pre-defined Activity or Transaction. For example loading a magnetic tape, accepting money at a point of sale, or reading data from a disk drive. |
| Operational | The lowest of three levels of Planning and delivery (Strategic, Tactical, Operational). Operational Activities include the day-to-day or short term Planning or delivery of a Business Process or IT Service Management Process. The term Operational is also a synonym for Live. |

| | |
|---|---|
| Operational Cost | Cost resulting from running the IT Services. Often repeating payments. For example staff costs, hardware maintenance and electricity (also known as "current expenditure" or "revenue expenditure"). See Capital Expenditure. |
| Operational Expenditure (OPEX) | Synonym for Operational Cost. |
| Operational Level Agreement (OLA) | (Service Design) (Continual Service Improvement) An Agreement between an IT Service Provider and another part of the same Organization. An OLA supports the IT Service Provider's delivery of IT Services to Customers. The OLA defines the goods or Services to be provided and the responsibilities of both parties. For example there could be an OLA<br>• between the IT Service Provider and a procurement department to obtain hardware in agreed times<br>• between the Service Desk and a Support Group to provide Incident Resolution in agreed times.<br>See Service Level Agreement. |
| Operations Bridge | (Service Operation) A physical location where IT Services and IT Infrastructure are monitored and managed. |
| Operations Control | Synonym for IT Operations Control. |
| Operations Management | Synonym for IT Operations Management. |
| Opportunity Cost | (Service Strategy) A Cost that is used in deciding between investment choices. Opportunity Cost represents the revenue that would have been generated by using the Resources in a different way. For example the Opportunity Cost of purchasing a new Server may include not carrying out a Service Improvement activity that the money could have been spent on. Opportunity cost analysis is used as part of a decision making processes, but is not treated as an actual Cost in any financial statement. |
| Optimize | Review, Plan and request Changes, in order to obtain the maximum Efficiency and Effectiveness from a Process, Configuration Item, Application etc. |
| Organization | A company, legal entity or other institution. Examples of Organizations that are not companies include International Standards Organization or itSMF. The term Organization is sometimes used to refer to any entity which has People, Resources and Budgets. For example a Project or Business Unit. |
| Outcome | The result of carrying out an Activity; following a Process; delivering an IT Service etc. The term Outcome is used to refer to intended results, as well as to actual results. See Objective. |
| Outsourcing | (Service Strategy) Using an External Service Provider to manage IT Services. See Service Sourcing, Type III Service Provider. |

| | |
|---|---|
| Overhead | Synonym for Indirect cost |
| Pain Value Analysis | (Service Operation) A technique used to help identify the Business Impact of one or more Problems. A formula is used to calculate Pain Value based on the number of Users affected, the duration of the Downtime, the Impact on each User, and the cost to the Business (if known). |
| Pareto Principle | (Service Operation) A technique used to priorities Activities. The Pareto Principle says that 80% of the value of any Activity is created with 20% of the effort. Pareto Analysis is also used in Problem Management to priorities possible Problem causes for investigation. |
| Partnership | A relationship between two Organizations which involves working closely together for common goals or mutual benefit. The IT Service Provider should have a Partnership with the Business, and with Third Parties who are critical to the delivery of IT Services. See Value Network. |
| Passive Monitoring | (Service Operation) Monitoring of a Configuration Item, an IT Service or a Process that relies on an Alert or notification to discover the current status. See Active Monitoring. |
| Pattern of Business Activity (PBA) | (Service Strategy) A Workload profile of one or more Business Activities. Patterns of Business Activity are used to help the IT Service Provider understand and plan for different levels of Business Activity. See User Profile. |
| Percentage utilization | (Service Design) The amount of time that a Component is busy over a given period of time. For example, if a CPU is busy for 1800 seconds in a one hour period, its utilization is 50% |
| Performance | A measure of what is achieved or delivered by a System, person, team, Process, or IT Service. |
| Performance Anatomy | (Service Strategy) An approach to Organizational Culture that integrates, and actively manages, leadership and strategy, people development, technology enablement, performance management and innovation. |
| Performance Management | (Continual Service Improvement) The Process responsible for day-to-day Capacity Management Activities. These include Monitoring, Threshold detection, Performance analysis and Tuning, and implementing Changes related to Performance and Capacity. |
| Pilot | (Service Transition) A limited Deployment of an IT Service, a Release or a Process to the Live Environment. A Pilot is used to reduce Risk and to gain User feedback and Acceptance. See Test, Evaluation. |

| | |
|---|---|
| Plan | A detailed proposal which describes the Activities and Resources needed to achieve an Objective. For example a Plan to implement a new IT Service or Process. ISO/IEC 20000 requires a Plan for the management of each IT Service Management Process. |
| Plan-Do-Check-Act | (Continual Service Improvement) A four stage cycle for Process management, attributed to Edward Deming. Plan-Do-Check-Act is also called the Deming Cycle. PLAN: Design or revise Processes that support the IT Services. DO: Implement the Plan and manage the Processes. CHECK: Measure the Processes and IT Services, compare with Objectives and produce reports ACT: Plan and implement Changes to improve the Processes. |
| Planned Downtime | (Service Design) Agreed time when an IT Service will not be available. Planned Downtime is often used for maintenance, upgrades and testing. See Change Window, Downtime. |
| Planning | An Activity responsible for creating one or more Plans. For example, Capacity Planning. |
| PMBOK | A Project management Standard maintained and published by the Project Management Institute. PMBOK stands for Project Management Body of Knowledge. See http://www.pmi.org/ for more information. See PRINCE2. |
| Policy | Formally documented management expectations and intentions. Policies are used to direct decisions, and to ensure consistent and appropriate development and implementation of Processes, Standards, Roles, Activities, IT Infrastructure etc. |
| Portable Facility | (Service Design) A prefabricated building, or a large vehicle, provided by a Third Party and moved to a site when needed by an IT Service Continuity Plan. See Recovery Option, Fixed Facility. |
| Post Implementation Review (PIR) | A Review that takes place after a Change or a Project has been implemented. A PIR determines if the Change or Project was successful, and identifies opportunities for improvement. |
| Practice | A way of working, or a way in which work must be done. Practices can include Activities, Processes, Functions, Standards and Guidelines. See Best Practice. |
| Prerequisite for Success (PFS) | An Activity that needs to be completed, or a condition that needs to be met, to enable successful implementation of a Plan or Process. A PFS is often an output from one Process that is a required input to another Process. |
| Pricing | (Service Strategy) The Activity for establishing how much Customers will be Charged. |

| | |
|---|---|
| PRINCE2 | The standard UK government methodology for Project management. See http://www.ogc.gov.uk/prince2/ for more information.<br>See PMBOK. |
| Priority | (Service Transition) (Service Operation) A Category used to identify the relative importance of an Incident, Problem or Change. Priority is based on Impact and Urgency, and is used to identify required times for actions to be taken. For example the SLA may state that Priority2 Incidents must be resolved within 12 hours. |
| Proactive Monitoring | (Service Operation) Monitoring that looks for patterns of Events to predict possible future Failures.<br>See Reactive Monitoring. |
| Proactive Problem Management | (Service Operation) Part of the Problem Management Process. The Objective of Proactive Problem Management is to identify Problems that might otherwise be missed. Proactive Problem Management analyses Incident Records, and uses data collected by other IT Service Management Processes to identify trends or significant Problems. |
| Problem | (Service Operation) A cause of one or more Incidents. The cause is not usually known at the time a Problem Record is created, and the Problem Management Process is responsible for further investigation. |
| Problem Management | (Service Operation) The Process responsible for managing the Lifecycle of all Problems. The primary Objectives of Problem Management are to prevent Incidents from happening, and to minimize the Impact of Incidents that cannot be prevented. |
| Problem Record | (Service Operation) A Record containing the details of a Problem. Each Problem Record documents the Lifecycle of a single Problem. |
| Procedure | A Document containing steps that specify how to achieve an Activity. Procedures are defined as part of Processes.<br>See Work Instruction. |
| Process | A structured set of Activities designed to accomplish a specific Objective. A Process takes one or more defined inputs and turns them into defined outputs. A Process may include any of the Roles, responsibilities, tools and management Controls required to reliably deliver the outputs. A Process may define Policies, Standards, Guidelines, Activities, and Work Instructions if they are needed. |
| Process Control | The Activity of planning and regulating a Process, with the Objective of performing the Process in an Effective, Efficient, and consistent manner. |

Process Manager
A Role responsible for Operational management of a Process. The Process Manager's responsibilities include Planning and coordination of all Activities required to carry out, monitor and report on the Process. There may be several Process Managers for one Process, for example regional Change Managers or IT Service Continuity Managers for each data centre. The Process Manager Role is often assigned to the person who carries out the Process Owner Role, but the two Roles may be separate in larger Organizations.

Process Owner
A Role responsible for ensuring that a Process is Fit for Purpose. The Process Owner's responsibilities include sponsorship, Design, Change Management and continual improvement of the Process and its Metrics. This Role is often assigned to the same person who carries out the Process Manager Role, but the two Roles may be separate in larger Organizations.

Production Environment
Synonym for Live Environment.

Profit Centre
(Service Strategy) A Business Unit which charges for Services provided. A Profit Centre can be created with the objective of making a profit, recovering Costs, or running at a loss. An IT Service Provider can be run as a Cost Centre or a Profit Centre.

pro-forma
A template, or example Document containing example data that will be replaced with the real values when these are available.

Program
A number of Projects and Activities that are planned and managed together to achieve an overall set of related Objectives and other Outcomes.

Project
A temporary Organization, with people and other Assets required to achieve an Objective or other Outcome. Each Project has a Lifecycle that typically includes initiation, Planning, execution, Closure etc. Projects are usually managed using a formal methodology such as PRINCE2.

Projected Service Outage (PSO)
(Service Transition) A Document that identifies the effect of planned Changes, maintenance Activities and Test Plans on agreed Service Levels.

PRojects IN Controlled Environments (PRINCE2)
See PRINCE2

Qualification
(Service Transition) An Activity that ensures that IT Infrastructure is appropriate, and correctly configured, to support an Application or IT Service.
See Validation.

| | |
|---|---|
| Quality | The ability of a product, Service, or Process to provide the intended value. For example, a hardware Component can be considered to be of high Quality if it performs as expected and delivers the required Reliability. Process Quality also requires an ability to monitor Effectiveness and Efficiency, and to improve them if necessary.<br>See Quality Management System. |
| Quality Assurance (QA) | (Service Transition) The Process responsible for ensuring that the Quality of a product, Service or Process will provide its intended Value. |
| Quality Management System (QMS) | (Continual Service Improvement) The set of Processes responsible for ensuring that all work carried out by an Organization is of a suitable Quality to reliably meet Business Objectives or Service Levels.<br>See ISO 9000. |
| Quick Win | (Continual Service Improvement) An improvement Activity which is expected to provide a Return on Investment in a short period of time with relatively small Cost and effort.<br>See Pareto Principle. |
| RACI | (Service Design) (Continual Service Improvement) A Model used to help define Roles and Responsibilities. RACI stands for Responsible, Accountable, Consulted and Informed.<br>See Stakeholder. |
| Reactive Monitoring | (Service Operation) Monitoring that takes action in response to an Event. For example submitting a batch job when the previous job completes, or logging an Incident when an Error occurs.<br>See Proactive Monitoring. |
| Reciprocal Arrangement | (Service Design) A Recovery Option. An agreement between two Organizations to share resources in an emergency. For example, Computer Room space or use of a mainframe. |
| Record | A Document containing the results or other output from a Process or Activity. Records are evidence of the fact that an Activity took place and may be paper or electronic. For example, an Audit report, an Incident Record, or the minutes of a meeting. |
| Recovery | (Service Design) (Service Operation) Returning a Configuration Item or an IT Service to a working state. Recovery of an IT Service often includes recovering data to a known consistent state. After Recovery, further steps may be needed before the IT Service can be made available to the Users (Restoration). |
| Recovery Option | (Service Design) A Strategy for responding to an interruption to Service. Commonly used Strategies are Do Nothing, Manual Workaround, Reciprocal Arrangement, Gradual Recovery, Intermediate Recovery, Fast Recovery, Immediate Recovery. Recovery Options may make use of dedicated facilities, or Third Party facilities shared by multiple Businesses. |

| | |
|---|---|
| Recovery Point Objective (RPO) | (Service Operation) The maximum amount of data that may be lost when Service is Restored after an interruption. Recovery Point Objective is expressed as a length of time before the Failure. For example a Recovery Point Objective of one day may be supported by daily Backups, and up to 24 hours of data may be lost. Recovery Point Objectives for each IT Service should be negotiated, agreed and documented, and used as Requirements for Service Design and IT Service Continuity Plans. |
| Recovery Time Objective (RTO) | (Service Operation) The maximum time allowed for recovery of an IT Service following an interruption. The Service Level to be provided may be less than normal Service Level Targets. Recovery Time Objectives for each IT Service should be negotiated, agreed and documented. See Business Impact Analysis. |
| Redundancy | Synonym for Fault Tolerance. The term Redundant also has a generic meaning of obsolete, or no longer needed. |
| Relationship | A connection or interaction between two people or things. In Business Relationship Management it is the interaction between the IT Service Provider and the Business. In Configuration Management it is a link between two Configuration Items that identifies a dependency or connection between them. For example Applications may be linked to the Servers they run on, IT Services have many links to all the CIs that contribute to them. |
| Relationship Processes | The ISO/IEC 20000 Process group that includes Business Relationship Management and Supplier Management. |
| Release | (Service Transition) A collection of hardware, software, documentation, Processes or other Components required to implement one or more approved Changes to IT Services. The contents of each Release are managed, Tested, and Deployed as a single entity. |
| Release and Deployment Management | (Service Transition) The Process responsible for both Release Management and Deployment. |
| Release Identification | (Service Transition) A naming convention used to uniquely identify a Release. The Release Identification typically includes a reference to the Configuration Item and a version number. For example Microsoft Office 2003 SR2. |
| Release Management | (Service Transition) The Process responsible for Planning, scheduling and controlling the movement of Releases to Test and Live Environments. The primary Objective of Release Management is to ensure that the integrity of the Live Environment is protected and that the correct Components are released. Release Management is part of the Release and Deployment Management Process. |
| Release Process | The name used by ISO/IEC 20000 for the Process group that includes Release Management. This group does not include any other Processes. Release Process is also used as a synonym for Release Management Process. |

| | |
|---|---|
| Release Record | (Service Transition) A Record in the CMDB that defines the content of a Release. A Release Record has Relationships with all Configuration Items that are affected by the Release. |
| Release Unit | (Service Transition) Components of an IT Service that are normally Released together. A Release Unit typically includes sufficient Components to perform a useful Function. For example one Release Unit could be a Desktop PC, including Hardware, Software, Licenses, Documentation etc. A different Release Unit may be the complete Payroll Application, including IT Operations Procedures and User training. |
| Release Window | Synonym for Change Window. |
| Reliability | (Service Design) (Continual Service Improvement) A measure of how long a Configuration Item or IT Service can perform its agreed Function without interruption. Usually measured as MTBF or MTBSI. The term Reliability can also be used to state how likely it is that a Process, Function etc. will deliver its required outputs. See Availability. |
| Remediation | (Service Transition) Recovery to a known state after a failed Change or Release. |
| Repair | (Service Operation) The replacement or correction of a failed Configuration Item. |
| Request for Change (RFC) | (Service Transition) A formal proposal for a Change to be made. An RFC includes details of the proposed Change, and may be recorded on paper or electronically. The term RFC is often misused to mean a Change Record, or the Change itself. |
| Request Fulfilment | (Service Operation) The Process responsible for managing the Lifecycle of all Service Requests. |
| Requirement | (Service Design) A formal statement of what is needed. For example a Service Level Requirement, a Project Requirement or the required Deliverables for a Process. See Statement of Requirements. |
| Resilience | (Service Design) The ability of a Configuration Item or IT Service to resist Failure or to Recover quickly following a Failure. For example, an armored cable will resist failure when put under stress. See Fault Tolerance. |
| Resolution | (Service Operation) Action taken to repair the Root Cause of an Incident or Problem, or to implement a Workaround. In ISO/IEC 20000, Resolution Processes is the Process group that includes Incident and Problem Management. |
| Resolution Processes | The ISO/IEC 20000 Process group that includes Incident Management and Problem Management. |

Resource                   (Service Strategy) A generic term that includes IT Infrastructure, people, money or
                           anything else that might help to deliver an IT Service. Resources are considered to
                           be Assets of an Organization.
                           See Capability, Service Asset.

Response Time              A measure of the time taken to complete an Operation or Transaction. Used in
                           Capacity Management as a measure of IT Infrastructure Performance, and in
                           Incident Management as a measure of the time taken to answer the phone, or to
                           start Diagnosis.

Responsiveness             A measurement of the time taken to respond to something. This could be
                           Response Time of a Transaction, or the speed with which an IT Service Provider
                           responds to an Incident or Request for Change etc.

Restoration of             See Restore.
Service

Restore                    (Service Operation) Taking action to return an IT Service to the Users after
                           Repair and Recovery from an Incident. This is the primary Objective of Incident
                           Management.

Retire                     (Service Transition) Permanent removal of an IT Service, or other Configuration
                           Item, from the Live Environment. Retired is a stage in the Lifecycle of many
                           Configuration Items.

Return on                  (Service Strategy) (Continual Service Improvement) A measurement of the
Investment (ROI)           expected benefit of an investment. In the simplest sense it is the net profit of an
                           investment divided by the net worth of the assets invested.
                           See Net Present Value, Value on Investment.

Return to Normal           (Service Design) The phase of an IT Service Continuity Plan during which full
                           normal operations are resumed. For example, if an alternate data centre has been
                           in use, then this phase will bring the primary data centre back into operation, and
                           restore the ability to invoke IT Service Continuity Plans again.

Review                     An evaluation of a Change, Problem, Process, Project etc. Reviews are typically
                           carried out at predefined points in the Lifecycle, and especially after Closure. The
                           purpose of a Review is to ensure that all Deliverables have been provided, and to
                           identify opportunities for improvement.
                           See Post Implementation Review.

Rights                     (Service Operation) Entitlements, or permissions, granted to a User or Role. For
                           example the Right to modify particular data, or to authorize a Change.

Risk                       A possible Event that could cause harm or loss, or affect the ability to achieve
                           Objectives. A Risk is measured by the probability of a Threat, the Vulnerability of
                           the Asset to that Threat, and the Impact it would have if it occurred.

| | |
|---|---|
| Risk Assessment | The initial steps of Risk Management. Analyzing the value of Assets to the business, identifying Threats to those Assets, and evaluating how Vulnerable each Asset is to those Threats. Risk Assessment can be quantitative (based on numerical data) or qualitative. |
| Risk Management | The Process responsible for identifying, assessing and controlling Risks. See Risk Assessment. |
| Role | A set of responsibilities, Activities and authorities granted to a person or team. A Role is defined in a Process. One person or team may have multiple Roles, for example the Roles of Configuration Manager and Change Manager may be carried out by a single person. |
| Rollout | (Service Transition) Synonym for Deployment. Most often used to refer to complex or phased Deployments or Deployments to multiple locations. |
| Root Cause | (Service Operation) The underlying or original cause of an Incident or Problem. |
| Root Cause Analysis (RCA) | (Service Operation) An Activity that identifies the Root Cause of an Incident or Problem. RCA typically concentrates on IT Infrastructure failures. See Service Failure Analysis. |
| Running Costs | Synonym for Operational Costs |
| Scalability | The ability of an IT Service, Process, Configuration Item etc. to perform its agreed Function when the Workload or Scope changes. |
| Scope | The boundary, or extent, to which a Process, Procedure, Certification, Contract etc. applies. For example the Scope of Change Management may include all Live IT Services and related Configuration Items, the Scope of an ISO/IEC 20000 Certificate may include all IT Services delivered out of a named data centre. |
| Second-line Support | (Service Operation) The second level in a hierarchy of Support Groups involved in the resolution of Incidents and investigation of Problems. Each level contains more specialist skills, or has more time or other Resources. |
| Security | See Information Security Management |
| Security Management | Synonym for Information Security Management |
| Security Policy | Synonym for Information Security Policy |
| Separation of Concerns (SoC) | (Service Strategy) An approach to Designing a solution or IT Service that divides the problem into pieces that can be solved independently. This approach separates "what" is to be done from "how" it is to be done. |
| Server | (Service Operation) A computer that is connected to a network and provides software Functions that are used by other computers. |
| Service | A means of delivering value to Customers by facilitating Outcomes Customers want to achieve without the ownership of specific Costs and Risks. |

| | |
|---|---|
| Service Acceptance Criteria (SAC) | (Service Transition) A set of criteria used to ensure that an IT Service meets its functionality and Quality Requirements and that the IT Service Provider is ready to Operate the new IT Service when it has been Deployed. See Acceptance. |
| Service Analytics | (Service Strategy) A technique used in the Assessment of the Business Impact of Incidents. Service Analytics Models the dependencies between Configuration Items, and the dependencies of IT Services on Configuration Items. |
| Service Asset | Any Capability or Resource of a Service Provider. See Asset. |
| Service Asset and Configuration Management (SACM) | (Service Transition) The Process responsible for both Configuration Management and Asset Management. |
| Service Capacity Management (SCM) | (Service Design) (Continual Service Improvement) The Activity responsible for understanding the Performance and Capacity of IT Services. The Resources used by each IT Service and the pattern of usage over time are collected, recorded, and analyzed for use in the Capacity Plan. See Business Capacity Management, Component Capacity Management. |
| Service Catalogue | (Service Design) A database or structured Document with information about all Live IT Services, including those available for Deployment. The Service Catalogue is the only part of the Service Portfolio published to Customers, and is used to support the sale and delivery of IT Services. The Service Catalogue includes information about deliverables, prices, contact points, ordering and request Processes. See Contract Portfolio. |
| Service Continuity Management | Synonym for IT Service Continuity Management. |
| Service Contract | (Service Strategy) A Contract to deliver one or more IT Services. The term Service Contract is also used to mean any Agreement to deliver IT Services, whether this is a legal Contract or an SLA. See Contract Portfolio. |
| Service Culture | A Customer oriented Culture. The major Objectives of a Service Culture are Customer satisfaction and helping the Customer to achieve their Business Objectives. |
| Service Design | (Service Design) A stage in the Lifecycle of an IT Service. Service Design includes a number of Processes and Functions and is the title of one of the Core ITIL publications. See Design. |

| | |
|---|---|
| Service Design Package | (Service Design) Document(s) defining all aspects of an IT Service and its Requirements through each stage of its Lifecycle. A Service Design Package is produced for each new IT Service, major Change, or IT Service Retirement. |
| Service Desk | (Service Operation) The Single Point of Contact between the Service Provider and the Users. A typical Service Desk manages Incidents and Service Requests, and also handles communication with the Users. |
| Service Failure Analysis (SFA) | (Service Design) An Activity that identifies underlying causes of one or more IT Service interruptions. SFA identifies opportunities to improve the IT Service Provider's Processes and tools, and not just the IT Infrastructure. SFA is a time constrained, project-like activity, rather than an ongoing process of analysis. See Root Cause Analysis. |
| Service Hours | (Service Design) (Continual Service Improvement) An agreed time period when a particular IT Service should be Available. For example, "Monday-Friday 08:00 to 17:00 except public holidays". Service Hours should be defined in a Service Level Agreement. |
| Service Improvement Plan (SIP) | (Continual Service Improvement) A formal Plan to implement improvements to a Process or IT Service. |
| Service Knowledge Management System (SKMS) | (Service Transition) A set of tools and databases that are used to manage knowledge and information. The SKMS includes the Configuration Management System, as well as other tools and databases. The SKMS stores, manages, updates, and presents all information that an IT Service Provider needs to manage the full Lifecycle of IT Services. |
| Service Level | Measured and reported achievement against one or more Service Level Targets. The term Service Level is sometimes used informally to mean Service Level Target. |
| Service Level Agreement (SLA) | (Service Design) (Continual Service Improvement) An Agreement between an IT Service Provider and a Customer. The SLA describes the IT Service, documents Service Level Targets, and specifies the responsibilities of the IT Service Provider and the Customer. A single SLA may cover multiple IT Services or multiple Customers. See Operational Level Agreement. |
| Service Level Management (SLM) | (Service Design) (Continual Service Improvement) The Process responsible for negotiating Service Level Agreements, and ensuring that these are met. SLM is responsible for ensuring that all IT Service Management Processes, Operational Level Agreements, and Underpinning Contracts, are appropriate for the agreed Service Level Targets. SLM monitors and reports on Service Levels, and holds regular Customer reviews. |

| Service Level Package (SLP) | (Service Strategy) A defined level of Utility and Warranty for a particular Service Package. Each SLP is designed to meet the needs of a particular Pattern of Business Activity. See Line of Service. |
|---|---|
| Service Level Requirement (SLR) | (Service Design) (Continual Service Improvement) A Customer Requirement for an aspect of an IT Service. SLRs are based on Business Objectives and are used to negotiate agreed Service Level Targets. |
| Service Level Target | (Service Design) (Continual Service Improvement) A commitment that is documented in a Service Level Agreement. Service Level Targets are based on Service Level Requirements, and are needed to ensure that the IT Service design is Fit for Purpose. Service Level Targets should be SMART, and are usually based on KPIs. |
| Service Maintenance Objective | (Service Operation) The expected time that a Configuration Item will be unavailable due to planned maintenance Activity. |
| Service Management | Service Management is a set of specialized organizational capabilities for providing value to customers in the form of services. |
| Service Management Lifecycle | An approach to IT Service Management that emphasizes the importance of coordination and Control across the various Functions, Processes, and Systems necessary to manage the full Lifecycle of IT Services. The Service Management Lifecycle approach considers the Strategy, Design, Transition, Operation and Continuous Improvement of IT Services. |
| Service Manager | A manager who is responsible for managing the end-to-end Lifecycle of one or more IT Services. The term Service Manager is also used to mean any manager within the IT Service Provider. Most commonly used to refer to a Business Relationship Manager, a Process Manager, an Account Manager or a senior manager with responsibility for IT Services overall. |
| Service Operation | (Service Operation) A stage in the Lifecycle of an IT Service. Service Operation includes a number of Processes and Functions and is the title of one of the Core ITIL publications. See Operation. |
| Service Owner | (Continual Service Improvement) A Role which is accountable for the delivery of a specific IT Service. |
| Service Package | (Service Strategy) A detailed description of an IT Service that is available to be delivered to Customers. A Service Package includes a Service Level Package and one or more Core Services and Supporting Services. |
| Service Pipeline | (Service Strategy) A database or structured Document listing all IT Services that are under consideration or Development, but are not yet available to Customers. The Service Pipeline provides a Business view of possible future IT Services and is part of the Service Portfolio which is not normally published to Customers. |

| | |
|---|---|
| Service Portfolio | (Service Strategy) The complete set of Services that are managed by a Service Provider. The Service Portfolio is used to manage the entire Lifecycle of all Services, and includes three Categories: Service Pipeline (proposed or in Development); Service Catalogue (Live or available for Deployment); and Retired Services. <br> See Service Portfolio Management, Contract Portfolio. |
| Service Portfolio Management (SPM) | (Service Strategy) The Process responsible for managing the Service Portfolio. Service Portfolio Management considers Services in terms of the Business value that they provide. |
| Service Potential | (Service Strategy) The total possible value of the overall Capabilities and Resources of the IT Service Provider. |
| Service Provider | (Service Strategy) An Organization supplying Services to one or more Internal Customers or External Customers. Service Provider is often used as an abbreviation for IT Service Provider. <br> See Type I Service Provider, Type II Service Provider, Type III Service Provider. |
| Service Provider Interface (SPI) | (Service Strategy) An interface between the IT Service Provider and a User, Customer, Business Process, or a Supplier. Analysis of Service Provider Interfaces helps to coordinate end-to-end management of IT Services. |
| Service Provisioning Optimization (SPO) | (Service Strategy) Analyzing the finances and constraints of an IT Service to decide if alternative approaches to Service delivery might reduce Costs or improve Quality. |
| Service Reporting | (Continual Service Improvement) The Process responsible for producing and delivering reports of achievement and trends against Service Levels. Service Reporting should agree the format, content and frequency of reports with Customers. |
| Service Request | (Service Operation) A request from a User for information, or advice, or for a Standard Change or for Access to an IT Service. For example to reset a password, or to provide standard IT Services for a new User. Service Requests are usually handled by a Service Desk, and do not require an RFC to be submitted. <br> See Request Fulfilment. |
| Service Sourcing | (Service Strategy) The Strategy and approach for deciding whether to provide a Service internally or to Outsource it to an External Service Provider. Service Sourcing also means the execution of this Strategy. <br> Service Sourcing includes: <br> • Internal Sourcing - Internal or Shared Services using Type I or Type II Service Providers. <br> • Traditional Sourcing - Full Service Outsourcing using a Type III Service Provider. <br> • Multivendor Sourcing - Prime, Consortium or Selective Outsourcing using Type III Service Providers. |

| | |
|---|---|
| Service Strategy | (Service Strategy) The title of one of the Core ITIL publications. Service Strategy establishes an overall Strategy for IT Services and for IT Service Management. |
| Service Transition | (Service Transition) A stage in the Lifecycle of an IT Service. Service Transition includes a number of Processes and Functions and is the title of one of the Core ITIL publications.<br>See Transition. |
| Service Utility | (Service Strategy) The Functionality of an IT Service from the Customer's perspective. The Business value of an IT Service is created by the combination of Service Utility (what the Service does) and Service Warranty (how well it does it).<br>See Utility. |
| Service Validation and Testing | (Service Transition) The Process responsible for Validation and Testing of a new or Changed IT Service. Service Validation and Testing ensures that the IT Service matches its Design Specification and will meet the needs of the Business. |
| Service Valuation | (Service Strategy) A measurement of the total Cost of delivering an IT Service, and the total value to the Business of that IT Service. Service Valuation is used to help the Business and the IT Service Provider agree on the value of the IT Service. |
| Service Warranty | (Service Strategy) Assurance that an IT Service will meet agreed Requirements. This may be a formal Agreement such as a Service Level Agreement or Contract, or may be a marketing message or brand image. The Business value of an IT Service is created by the combination of Service Utility (what the Service does) and Service Warranty (how well it does it).<br>See Warranty. |
| Serviceability | (Service Design) (Continual Service Improvement) The ability of a Third Party Supplier to meet the terms of their Contract. This Contract will include agreed levels of Reliability, Maintainability or Availability for a Configuration Item. |
| Shift | (Service Operation) A group or team of people who carry out a specific Role for a fixed period of time. For example there could be four shifts of IT Operations Control personnel to support an IT Service that is used 24 hours a day. |
| Simulation modeling | (Service Design) (Continual Service Improvement) A technique that creates a detailed Model to predict the behavior of a Configuration Item or IT Service. Simulation Models can be very accurate but are expensive and time consuming to create. A Simulation Model is often created by using the actual Configuration Items that are being modeled, with artificial Workloads or Transactions. They are used in Capacity Management when accurate results are important. A simulation model is sometimes called a Performance Benchmark. |
| Single Point of Contact | (Service Operation) Providing a single consistent way to communicate with an Organization or Business Unit. For example, a Single Point of Contact for an IT Service Provider is usually called a Service Desk. |

| | |
|---|---|
| Single Point of Failure (SPOF) | (Service Design) Any Configuration Item that can cause an Incident when it fails, and for which a Countermeasure has not been implemented. A SPOF may be a person, or a step in a Process or Activity, as well as a Component of the IT Infrastructure.<br>See Failure. |
| SLAM Chart | (Continual Service Improvement) A Service Level Agreement Monitoring Chart is used to help monitor and report achievements against Service Level Targets. A SLAM Chart is typically color coded to show whether each agreed Service Level Target has been met, missed, or nearly missed during each of the previous 12 months. |
| SMART | (Service Design) (Continual Service Improvement) An acronym for helping to remember that targets in Service Level Agreements and Project Plans should be Specific, Measurable, Achievable, Relevant and Timely. |
| Snapshot | (Service Transition) The current state of a Configuration as captured by a discovery tool.<br>Also used as a synonym for Benchmark.<br>See Baseline. |
| Source | See Service Sourcing. |
| Specification | A formal definition of Requirements. A Specification may be used to define technical or Operational Requirements, and may be internal or external.<br>Many public Standards consist of a Code of Practice and a Specification. The Specification defines the Standard against which an Organization can be Audited. |
| Stakeholder | All people who have an interest in an Organization, Project, IT Service etc. Stakeholders may be interested in the Activities, targets, Resources, or Deliverables. Stakeholders may include Customers, Partners, employees, shareholders, owners, etc.<br>See RACI. |
| Standard | A mandatory Requirement. Examples include ISO/IEC 20000 (an international Standard), an internal security Standard for Unix configuration, or a government Standard for how financial Records should be maintained. The term Standard is also used to refer to a Code of Practice or Specification published by a Standards Organization such as ISO or BSI.<br>See Guideline. |
| Standard Change | (Service Transition) A pre-approved Change that is low Risk, relatively common and follows a Procedure or Work Instruction. For example password reset or provision of standard equipment to a new employee. RFCs are not required to implement a Standard Change, and they are logged and tracked using a different mechanism, such as a Service Request.<br>See Change Model. |

| | |
|---|---|
| Standard Operating Procedures (SOP) | (Service Operation) Procedures used by IT Operations Management. |
| Standby | (Service Design) Used to refer to Resources that are not required to deliver the Live IT Services, but are available to support IT Service Continuity Plans. For example a Standby data centre may be maintained to support Hot Standby, Warm Standby or Cold Standby arrangements. |
| Statement of requirements (SOR) | (Service Design) A Document containing all Requirements for a product purchase, or a new or changed IT Service. See Terms of Reference. |
| Status | The name of a required field in many types of Record. It shows the current stage in the Lifecycle of the associated Configuration Item, Incident, Problem etc. |
| Status Accounting | (Service Transition) The Activity responsible for recording and reporting the Lifecycle of each Configuration Item. |
| Storage Management | (Service Operation) The Process responsible for managing the storage and maintenance of data throughout its Lifecycle. |
| Strategic | (Service Strategy) The highest of three levels of Planning and delivery (Strategic, Tactical, Operational). Strategic Activities include Objective setting and long term Planning to achieve the overall Vision. |
| Strategy | (Service Strategy) A Strategic Plan designed to achieve defined Objectives. |
| Super User | (Service Operation) A User who helps other Users, and assists in communication with the Service Desk or other parts of the IT Service Provider. Super Users typically provide support for minor Incidents and training. |
| Supplier | (Service Strategy) (Service Design) A Third Party responsible for supplying goods or Services that are required to deliver IT services. Examples of suppliers include commodity hardware and software vendors, network and telecom providers, and Outsourcing Organizations. See Underpinning Contract, Supply Chain. |
| Supplier and Contract Database (SCD) | (Service Design) A database or structured Document used to manage Supplier Contracts throughout their Lifecycle. The SCD contains key Attributes of all Contracts with Suppliers, and should be part of the Service Knowledge Management System. |
| Supplier Management | (Service Design) The Process responsible for ensuring that all Contracts with Suppliers support the needs of the Business, and that all Suppliers meet their contractual commitments. |
| Supply Chain | (Service Strategy) The Activities in a Value Chain carried out by Suppliers. A Supply Chain typically involves multiple Suppliers, each adding value to the product or Service. See Value Network. |

| Support Group | (Service Operation) A group of people with technical skills. Support Groups provide the Technical Support needed by all of the IT Service Management Processes.<br>See Technical Management. |
| Support Hours | (Service Design) (Service Operation) The times or hours when support is available to the Users. Typically this is the hours when the Service Desk is available. Support Hours should be defined in a Service Level Agreement, and may be different from Service Hours. For example, Service Hours may be 24 hours a day, but the Support Hours may be 07:00 to 19:00. |
| Supporting Service | (Service Strategy) A Service that enables or enhances a Core Service. For example a Directory Service or a Backup Service.<br>See Service Package. |
| SWOT Analysis | (Continual Service Improvement) A technique that reviews and analyses the internal strengths and weaknesses of an Organization and the external opportunities and threats which it faces SWOT stands for Strengths, Weaknesses, Opportunities and Threats. |
| System | A number of related things that work together to achieve an overall Objective. For example:<br>• A computer System including hardware, software and Applications.<br>• A management System, including multiple Processes that are planned and managed together. For example a Quality Management System.<br>• A Database Management System or Operating System that includes many software modules that are designed to perform a set of related Functions. |
| System Management | The part of IT Service Management that focuses on the management of IT Infrastructure rather than Process. |
| Tactical | The middle of three levels of Planning and delivery (Strategic, Tactical, Operational). Tactical Activities include the medium term Plans required to achieve specific Objectives, typically over a period of weeks to months. |
| Tag | (Service Strategy) A short code used to identify a Category. For example tags EC1, EC2, EC3 etc. might be used to identify different Customer outcomes when analyzing and comparing Strategies. The term Tag is also used to refer to the Activity of assigning Tags to things. |
| Technical Management | (Service Operation) The Function responsible for providing technical skills in support of IT Services and management of the IT Infrastructure. Technical Management defines the Roles of Support Groups, as well as the tools, Processes and Procedures required. |
| Technical Observation (TO) | (Continual Service Improvement) A technique used in Service Improvement, Problem investigation and Availability Management. Technical support staff meet to monitor the behavior and Performance of an IT Service and make recommendations for improvement. |

| Technical Service | Synonym for Infrastructure Service. |
| Technical Support | Synonym for Technical Management. |
| Tension Metrics | (Continual Service Improvement) A set of related Metrics, in which improvements to one Metric have a negative effect on another. Tension Metrics are designed to ensure that an appropriate balance is achieved. |
| Terms of Reference (TOR) | (Service Design) A Document specifying the Requirements, Scope, Deliverables, Resources and schedule for a Project or Activity. |
| Test | (Service Transition) An Activity that verifies that a Configuration Item, IT Service, Process, etc. meets its Specification or agreed Requirements. See Service Validation and Testing, Acceptance. |
| Test Environment | (Service Transition) A controlled Environment used to Test Configuration Items, Builds, IT Services, Processes etc. |
| Third Party | A person, group, or Business who is not part of the Service Level Agreement for an IT Service, but is required to ensure successful delivery of that IT Service. For example a software Supplier, a hardware maintenance company, or a facilities department. Requirements for Third Parties are typically specified in Underpinning Contracts or Operational Level Agreements. |
| Third-line Support | (Service Operation) The third level in a hierarchy of Support Groups involved in the resolution of Incidents and investigation of Problems. Each level contains more specialist skills, or has more time or other Resources. |
| Threat | Anything that might exploit a Vulnerability. Any potential cause of an Incident can be considered to be a Threat. For example a fire is a Threat that could exploit the Vulnerability of flammable floor coverings. This term is commonly used in Information Security Management and IT Service Continuity Management, but also applies to other areas such as Problem and Availability Management. |
| Threshold | The value of a Metric which should cause an Alert to be generated, or management action to be taken. For example "Priority1 Incident not solved within 4 hours", "more than 5 soft disk errors in an hour", or "more than 10 failed changes in a month". |
| Throughput | (Service Design) A measure of the number of Transactions, or other Operations, performed in a fixed time. For example 5000 emails sent per hour, or 200 disk I/Os per second. |
| Total Cost of Ownership (TCO) | (Service Strategy) A methodology used to help make investment decisions. TCO assesses the full Lifecycle Cost of owning a Configuration Item, not just the initial Cost or purchase price. See Total Cost of Utilization. |

| | |
|---|---|
| Total Cost of Utilization (TCU) | (Service Strategy) A methodology used to help make investment and Service Sourcing decisions. TCU assesses the full Lifecycle Cost to the Customer of using an IT Service.<br>See Total Cost of Ownership. |
| Total Quality Management (TQM) | (Continual Service Improvement) A methodology for managing continual Improvement by using a Quality Management System. TQM establishes a Culture involving all people in the Organization in a Process of continual monitoring and improvement. |
| Transaction | A discrete Function performed by an IT Service. For example transferring money from one bank account to another. A single Transaction may involve numerous additions, deletions and modifications of data. Either all of these complete successfully or none of them is carried out. |
| Transition | (Service Transition) A change in state, corresponding to a movement of an IT Service or other Configuration Item from one Lifecycle status to the next. |
| Transition Planning and Support | (Service Transition) The Process responsible for Planning all Service Transition Processes and co-coordinating the resources that they require. These Service Transition Processes are Change Management, Service Asset and Configuration Management, Release and Deployment Management, Service Validation and Testing, Evaluation, and Knowledge Management. |
| Trend Analysis | (Continual Service Improvement) Analysis of data to identify time related patterns. Trend Analysis is used in Problem Management to identify common Failures or fragile Configuration Items, and in Capacity Management as a Modeling tool to predict future behavior. It is also used as a management tool for identifying deficiencies in IT Service Management Processes. |
| Tuning | The Activity responsible for Planning Changes to make the most efficient use of Resources. Tuning is part of Performance Management, which also includes Performance Monitoring and implementation of the required Changes. |
| Type I Service Provider | (Service Strategy) An Internal Service Provider that is embedded within a Business Unit. There may be several Type I Service Providers within an Organization. |
| Type II Service Provider | (Service Strategy) An Internal Service Provider that provides shared IT Services to more than one Business Unit. |
| Type III Service Provider | (Service Strategy) A Service Provider that provides IT Services to External Customers. |
| Underpinning Contract (UC) | (Service Design) A Contract between an IT Service Provider and a Third Party. The Third Party provides goods or Services that support delivery of an IT Service to a Customer. The Underpinning Contract defines targets and responsibilities that are required to meet agreed Service Level Targets in an SLA. |

| Unit Cost | (Service Strategy) The Cost to the IT Service Provider of providing a single Component of an IT Service. For example the Cost of a single desktop PC, or of a single Transaction. |

| Urgency | (Service Transition) (Service Design) A measure of how long it will be until an Incident, Problem or Change has a significant Impact on the Business. For example a high Impact Incident may have low Urgency, if the Impact will not affect the Business until the end of the financial year. Impact and Urgency are used to assign Priority. |

| Usability | (Service Design) The ease with which an Application, product, or IT Service can be used. Usability Requirements are often included in a Statement of Requirements. |

| Use Case | (Service Design) A technique used to define required functionality and Objectives, and to Design Tests. Use Cases define realistic scenarios that describe interactions between Users and an IT Service or other System. See Change Case. |

| User | A person who uses the IT Service on a day-to-day basis. Users are distinct from Customers, as some Customers do not use the IT Service directly. |

| User Profile (UP) | (Service Strategy) A pattern of User demand for IT Services. Each User Profile includes one or more Patterns of Business Activity. |

| Utility | (Service Strategy) Functionality offered by a Product or Service to meet a particular need. Utility is often summarized as "what it does". See Service Utility. |

| Validation | (Service Transition) An Activity that ensures a new or changed IT Service, Process, Plan, or other Deliverable meets the needs of the Business. Validation ensures that Business Requirements are met even though these may have changed since the original Design. See Verification, Acceptance, Qualification, Service Validation and Testing. |

| Value Chain | (Service Strategy) A sequence of Processes that creates a product or Service that is of value to a Customer. Each step of the sequence builds on the previous steps and contributes to the overall product or Service. See Value Network. |

| Value for Money | An informal measure of Cost Effectiveness. Value for Money is often based on a comparison with the Cost of alternatives. See Cost Benefit Analysis. |

| Value Network | (Service Strategy) A complex set of Relationships between two or more groups or organizations. Value is generated through exchange of knowledge, information, goods or Services. See Value Chain, Partnership. |

| | |
|---|---|
| Value on Investment (VOI) | (Continual Service Improvement) A measurement of the expected benefit of an investment. VOI considers both financial and intangible benefits. See Return on Investment. |
| Variable Cost | (Service Strategy) A Cost that depends on how much the IT Service is used, how many products are produced, the number and type of Users, or something else that cannot be fixed in advance. See Variable Cost Dynamics. |
| Variable Cost Dynamics | (Service Strategy) A technique used to understand how overall Costs are impacted by the many complex variable elements that contribute to the provision of IT Services. |
| Variance | The difference between a planned value and the actual measured value. Commonly used in Financial Management, Capacity Management and Service Level Management, but could apply in any area where Plans are in place. |
| Verification | (Service Transition) An Activity that ensures a new or changed IT Service, Process, Plan, or other Deliverable is complete, accurate, Reliable and matches its Design Specification. See Validation, Acceptance, Service Validation and Testing. |
| Verification and Audit | (Service Transition) The Activities responsible for ensuring that information in the CMDB is accurate and that all Configuration Items have been identified and recorded in the CMDB. Verification includes routine checks that are part of other Processes. For example, verifying the serial number of a desktop PC when a User logs an Incident. Audit is a periodic, formal check. |
| Version | (Service Transition) A Version is used to identify a specific Baseline of a Configuration Item. Versions typically use a naming convention that enables the sequence or date of each Baseline to be identified. For example Payroll Application Version 3 contains updated functionality from Version 2. |
| Vision | A description of what the Organization intends to become in the future. A Vision is created by senior management and is used to help influence Culture and Strategic Planning. |
| Vital Business Function (VBF) | (Service Design) A Function of a Business Process which is critical to the success of the Business. Vital Business Functions are an important consideration of Business Continuity Management, IT Service Continuity Management and Availability Management. |
| Vulnerability | A weakness that could be exploited by a Threat. For example an open firewall port, a password that is never changed, or a flammable carpet. A missing Control is also considered to be a Vulnerability. |
| Warm Standby | Synonym for Intermediate Recovery. |

Warranty

(Service Strategy) A promise or guarantee that a product or Service will meet its agreed Requirements.
See Service Validation and Testing, Service Warranty.

Work in Progress (WIP)

A Status that means Activities have started but are not yet complete. It is commonly used as a Status for Incidents, Problems, Changes etc.

Work Instruction

A Document containing detailed instructions that specify exactly what steps to follow to carry out an Activity. A Work Instruction contains much more detail than a Procedure and is only created if very detailed instructions are needed.

Workaround

(Service Operation) Reducing or eliminating the Impact of an Incident or Problem for which a full Resolution is not yet available. For example by restarting a failed Configuration Item. Workarounds for Problems are documented in Known Error Records. Workarounds for Incidents that do not have associated Problem Records are documented in the Incident Record.

Workload

The Resources required to deliver an identifiable part of an IT Service. Workloads may be Categorized by Users, groups of Users, or Functions within the IT Service. This is used to assist in analyzing and managing the Capacity, Performance and Utilization of Configuration Items and IT Services. The term Workload is sometimes used as a synonym for Throughput.

# Acronyms

| | |
|---|---|
| AMIS | Availability Management Information System |
| APMG | APM Group |
| BCM | Business Continuity Management |
| BCP | Business Continuity Plan |
| BCS | British Computer Society |
| BIA | Business Impact Analysis |
| BPO | Business Process Outsourcing |
| BU | Business Unit |
| CAB | Change Advisory Board |
| CCM | Component Capacity Management |
| CFIA | Component Failure Impact Analysis |
| CI | Configuration Item |
| CMDB | Configuration Management Database |
| CMIS | Capacity Management Information System |
| CMS | Configuration Management System |
| CS | Change Schedule |
| CSF | Critical Success Factor |
| CSI | Continual Service Improvement |
| CSP | Core Service Package |
| DIKW | Data Information Knowledge Wisdom |
| DML | Definitive Media Library |
| ECAB | Emergency Change Advisory Board |
| ELS | Early Life Support |
| FTA | Fault Tree Analysis |
| HR | Human Resources |
| ISMS | Information Security Management System |
| ITIL | Information Technology Infrastructure Library |
| ITSCM | IT Service Continuity Management |
| itSMF | IT Service Management Forum |
| KEDB | Known Error Database |
| KPI | Key Performance Indicator |
| KPO | Knowledge Process Outsourcing |
| LCS | Loyalist Certification Services |

| | |
|---|---|
| LOS | Line of Service |
| M_o_R | Management of Risk |
| MTBF | Mean Time Between Failures |
| MTBSI | Mean Time Between Service Incidents |
| MTTR | Mean Time To Repair |
| MTRS | Mean Time to Restore Service |
| OGC | Office of Government Commerce |
| OLA | Operational Level Agreement |
| PBA | Pattern of Business Activity |
| PDCA | Plan Do Check Act |
| PFS | Prerequisites for Success |
| PIR | Post-Implementation Review |
| PRINCE2 | PRojects IN Controlled Environments |
| PSA | Projected Service Availability |
| PSO | Projected Service Outage |
| RAD | Rapid Application Development |
| RFC | Request for Change |
| SAC | Service Acceptance Criteria |
| SACM | Service Asset and Configuration Management |
| SCD | Supplier and Contract Database |
| SCM | Service Catalogue Management |
| SDP | Service Design Package |
| SFA | Service Failure Analysis |
| SIP | Service Improvement Plan |
| SKMS | Service Knowledge Management System |
| SLA | Service Level Agreement |
| SLM | Service Level Management |
| SLP | Service Level Package |
| SLR | Service Level Requirement |
| SoC | Separation of Concerns |
| SPM | Service Portfolio Management |
| SPOC | Single Point of Contact |
| SPOF | Single Point of Failure |
| TCU | Total Cost of Utilization |
| TSO | The Stationary Office |
| UC | Underpinning Contract |
| VBF | Vital Business Function |
| VCD | Variable Cost Dynamics |

# References

APM Group Website. http://www.apmgroup.co.uk

Bon, J. van, (Ed.) (2007). *Foundations of IT Service Management, Based on ITIL V3.* Zaltbommel: Van Haren Publishing for itSMF.

Bon, J. van, (Ed.) (2007). *IT Service Management, Based on ITIL V3.- A Pocket Guide.* Zaltbommel: Van Haren Publishing

*ITIL. Continual Service Improvement* (2007). OGC. London: TSO.

*ITIL. Service Design* (2007). OGC. London: TSO.

*ITIL. Service Operation* (2007). OGC. London: TSO.

*ITIL. Service Strategy* (2007). OGC. London: TSO.

*ITIL. Service Transition* (2007). OGC. London: TSO.

*ITIL Service Management Practices V3 Qualification Scheme* (2007). APM Group

The Official ITIL Site, http://www.itil-officialsite.com

*The ITIL V3 Foundation Certificate in IT Service Management SYLLABUS*, Version 3.1. APM Group London

# Index

# ITIL Books

## Foundations of ITIL®V3

Now updated to encompass all of the implications of the V3 refresh of ITIL, the new V3 Foundations book looks at Best Practices, focusing on the Lifecycle approach, and covering the ITIL Service Lifecycle, processes and functions for Service Strategy, Service Design, Service Operation, Service Transition and Continual Service Improvement.

English
€39.95
excl tax

ISBN 978 90 8753 057 0   (english edition)

## ITIL® V3 Foundation Exam: The Study Guide

A complete and thorough explanation of all key concepts for ITIL V3 Foundation Exam, this title contains official sample exams and glossary of terms. Endorsed by APMG, it is definitely a great fold-flat format for class training or self-study.

English
€22.50
excl tax

ISBN 978 90 8753 069 3   (english edition)

## ITIL®V3 - A Pocket Guide

A concise summary for ITIL®V3, providing a quick and portable reference tool to this leading set of best practices for IT Service Management.

English
€15.95
excl tax

ISBN 978 90 8753 102 7   (english edition)

Van Haren Publishing is a leading international publisher, specializing in best practice titles for IT management and business management. Van Haren Publishing publishes in 14 languages, and has sales and distribution agents in over 40 countries worldwide: www.vanharen.net

# ISO/IEC 20000

### ISO/IEC 20000: An Introduction

Promoting awareness of the certification for organizations within the IT Service Management environment.

ISBN 978 90 8753 081 5 (english edition)

English
€49.95
excl tax

### Implementing ISO/IEC 20000 Certification: The Roadmap

Practical advice, to assist readers through the requirements of the standard, the scoping, the project approach, the certification procedure and management of the certification.

ISBN 978 90 8753 082 2 (english edition)

English
€39.95
excl tax

### ISO/IEC 20000: A Pocket Guide

A quick and accessible guide to the fundamental requirements for corporate certification.

ISBN 978 90 77212 79 0 (english edition)

English
€15.95
excl tax

# Other leading ITSM Books